CW01238679

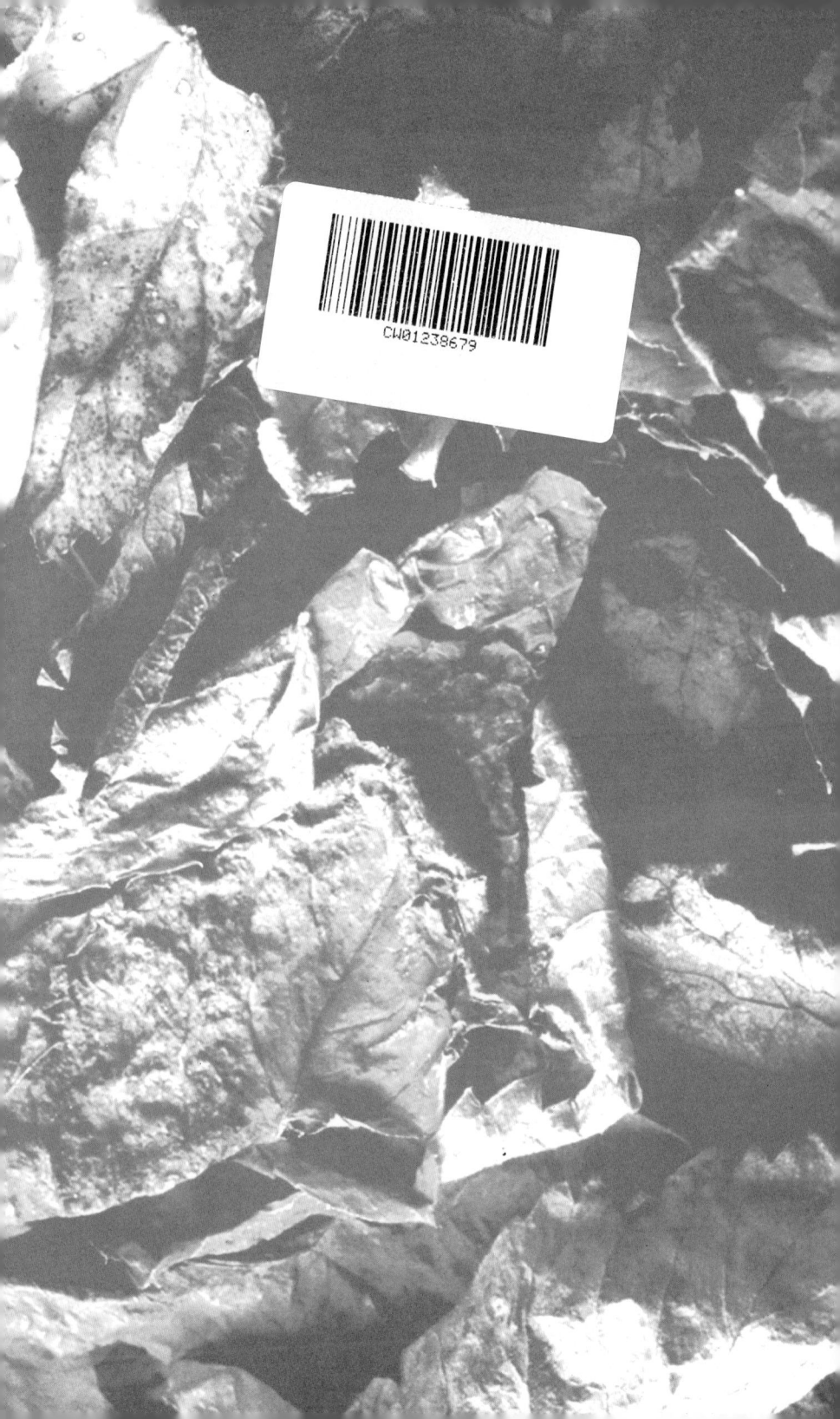

WESTERN GHATS

BIODIVERSITY • PEOPLE • CONSERVATION

Rupa & Co

Copyright © R.J. Ranjit Daniels & Jayshree Vencatesan 2008

Published 2008 by

Rupa & Co

7/16, Ansari Road, Daryaganj
New Delhi 110 002

Sales Centres:
Allahabad Bangalooru Chandigarh Chennai
Hyderabad Jaipur Kathmandu
Kolkata Mumbai Pune

All rights reserved.
No part of this publication may be reproduced,
stored in a retrieval system, or transmitted in
any form or by any means, electronic,
mechanical, photocopying, recording or otherwise,
without the prior permission of the publishers.

Designed & typeset by
PealiDezine
peali@pealidezine.com

Printed in India by
Gopsons Papers Ltd., Noida

Dedicated to

Professor Madhav Gadgil
Professor M.K. Prasad
and
Dr Satis Chandra Nair

for their pioneering and sustained efforts
in conserving the biodiversity and the people of the
Western Ghats

Content

PREFACE	viii
ORIGINS	2
From Gondwanaland to Asia	2
GEOGRAPHY	8
A Landscape Unsurpassed	8
FLORA AND FAUNA	14
Of Creatures Great and Small	14
Rusts, Mildew and Mushrooms	15
Plants	17
Insects	24
Arthropods other than Insects	35
Snails, Leeches and Worms	39
Fishes	42
Frogs, Toads and Caecilians	45
Turtles, Lizards and Snakes	49
Birds	53
Mammals	58
Living Communities	61
Flowering Plant Communities	63
Ant Communities	67
Butterfly Communities	67
Fish Communities	68
Amphibian Communities	70
Reptile Communities	71
Bird Communities	73
Mammal Communities	74
Ecological Patterns	75

PEOPLE, CULTURE AND HISTORY	77
The First Human Invaders	77
Cultural Landscapes	79
From Monarchs to the British Raj	83
HUMAN ACTIVITY AND ECOLOGICAL CHANGE	90
Taming the Wilderness	99
Gardens that Spread	95
Muddy Waters	99
Thorns and Vermin	102
Cattle that Devour	107
Man and Beast in Conflict	109
The Survivors	113
Constrained by Development	117
LOOKING AHEAD	124
What's on the Horizon?	124
SOURCES OF INFORMATION	138

WESTERN GHATS | vii

Preface

Peninsular India is endowed with a set of hill ranges that run largely along its periphery. The Vindhya and Satpura ranges in the north connect these hill ranges, forming a triangle that encloses the Deccan Plateau. Western Ghats is a 1,600 kilometre long chain of hills that runs along the western coastal plains, starting from the Surat Dangs in south-western Gujarat, passing through western Maharashtra along Pune and Satara, through Goa and then Belgaum in northern Karnataka, spreading east till the Billigiri Rangana Temple (BRT) Hills in the Mysore Plateau, then further south through Kerala till around Coimbatore and east closer to Madurai, before going down to Kanyakumari in Tamil Nadu.

A number of ecologically distinct segments have been identified traditionally and are known by different local names; for example, Sahyadri Hills, Bababudan Hills, Nilgiri Hills, Palani Hills, Anaimalai Hills, Meghamalai Hills, High Wavy Mountains, Grass Hills, High Ranges and Agasthyamalai Hills. The local names are hybrid in nature and represent the great diversity of languages spoken throughout the long hill chain that links the six south Indian states. In fact, the name Western Ghats is also a hybrid—an inverted binomial name, in which the specific name denoting its geographical position is in English, whereas the generic name is derived from the Sanskrit word for hills.

The geological processes that gave rise to the Western Ghats are the same that were responsible for the creation of at least a part of the Eastern Ghats—the hill ranges in central Tamil Nadu and eastern Andhra Pradesh—as well as Sri Lanka. As a result, these hills are geologically similar in a number of ways and share many species of endemic plants and animals. Sri Lanka, thanks to its largely equatorial climate, has retained a good part of the tropical rainforest and its associated biodiversity whereas the eastern hills of southern India have lost much of their original

A Panoramic View of the Western Ghats

flora and fauna due to the progressively drier conditions.

However, similarities in the biodiversity of the Western Ghats and Sri Lanka have long drawn the attention of biogeographers. Almost a hundred years before Norman Myers treated the two together as one of the world's twenty-five biodiversity hotspots, W.T. Blanford, an early British naturalist, had classified them as belonging to a single biogeographically homogeneous unit: the Indo-Ceylonese Province. Varying altitude, changing aspect, and the resultant variations in rainfall have together rendered these hills as one of the world's most unique and diverse biogeographical provinces. Tropical hills similar to these are found only in Madagascar and in Queensland in Australia.

Efforts to conserve the biodiversity of the Western Ghats can be traced far back into history. Such efforts began with a rather narrow focus on plants like teak and sandalwood, and animals such as the elephant, but soon widened in scope to demarcate biodiversity-rich landscapes as Protected Areas. Silent Valley, a pristine landscape in the Western Ghats of Kerala, earlier earmarked for a hydro-electric project, was declared a National Park—a landmark initiative of the Government of India that placed the value of a tropical rainforest ecosystem in the country, and its endemic biodiversity, above short-term human goals. Today, Silent Valley is just one among nearly sixty landscapes in the Western Ghats that enjoy the status of Protected Area (PA).

This angry elephant almost trampled our vehicle!

A countrywide effort was launched by the Ministry of Environment and Forests (MoEF) of the Government of India in the year 2000 to prepare the National Biodiversity Strategy and Action Plan (NBSAP), in order to fulfil its commitment to the Convention on Biological Diversity. The project was coordinated by Kalpavriksh and overseen by a Technical Committee. NBSAP was designed to be a document consolidated from sub-plans prepared at the eco-regional, state, and sub-state levels. At the eco-regional level, an exclusive plan was developed for the Western Ghats. Over two hundred institutions and individuals participated in the process of drafting the Action Plan and contributed to it in various ways. The draft plan was submitted to MoEF in 2001 and endorsed the next year.

This book is a result of the experience we gained in coordinating the drafting of the Action Plan and a response to the felt need for a comprehensive reference book on the Western Ghats, its biodiversity, its people, and the challenge of conservation. While preparing the Action Plan we had the opportunity to read and review over 150 published and unpublished documents concerning biodiversity in general and the Western Ghats in particular. Much of the published literature available has been consulted in preparing this book, and updated with the data we have personally gathered in the recent years. Many friends have been kind to share unpublished information and photographs on the biodiversity and people of the Western Ghats, and we have acknowledged them throughout the text.

Besides the financial support that MoEF provided for the preparation of the Biodiversity Strategy and Action Plan, we benefited from grants provided by a couple of other agencies to carry out field research in the Western Ghats since 2002. A research project on the impact of pesticides on the amphibians of the Western Ghats, supported by a one-year seed grant from the Declining Amphibian Populations Task Force (DAPTF) of the IUCN, gave us the opportunity to work at Valparai in the

Anaimalai Hills, and, among other things, study the various dimensions of human-animal conflicts in landscapes highly impacted by human activity. More recently, the Smithsonian Tropical Research Institution through its Centre for Tropical Forest Studies funded a six-month post-doctoral study on the role of forest reserves as refugia for human-impacted plants in Mudumalai Wildlife Sanctuary. This study gave us the opportunity to obtain first hand information on the complexities of human-animal conflicts, especially where large mammals are concerned, and on human livelihoods and Protected Area management in the Western Ghats.

The Periyar Foundation (Thekkady, Kerala) invited us in 2006 to travel through the Periyar Tiger Reserve and the adjoining High Wavy Mountains and Meghamalai Ranges in the southern Western Ghats. Further, a three-month survey of the status of the Nilgiri Tahr in collaboration with the Wildlife Trust of India gave us more opportunities to travel and study the

The typical mosaic of lowland forests and secondary grasslands

biodiversity, the people and challenges of conservation in the southern Western Ghats.

We profusely thank the local residents in and around the Mudumalai Wildlife Sanctuary for having supported us in a number of ways, especially while drafting the Biodiversity Strategy and Action Plan. We wish to specifically acknowledge the support provided by the Chennai Snake Park, the Zoological Survey of India (Chennai), the Tamil Nadu Forest Department, the State Forest Service College (Coimbatore), the Kerala Forest Department, the Kerala Forest Research Institute, the Karnataka Forest Department, the Centre for Ecological Sciences of the Indian Institute of Science (Bangalore and field stations at Masinagudi and Kumta), the American College (Madurai), the Tata Tea Estates (Valparai), the Anaimalais Biodiversity Conservation Association (Valparai), and the United Planters' Association of South India (Valparai). A number of friends have contributed illustrations and photographs for the book. We are grateful to each one of them, and where the illustrations and photographs have been used, the contributor has been specifically acknowledged.

No book can fully deal with the Western Ghats, its biodiversity, its people, and the conservation challenges. This book is just a beginning, meant to be an eye-opener and a source of inspiration to all who read it. And, therefore, we have tried our best to keep the language simple by avoiding most ecological jargon. It is our sincere wish that this book serves as a comprehensive source of information to all those interested in the conservation of biodiversity in the Western Ghats.

R.J. Ranjit Daniels
Jayshree Vencatesan
December 2006, Chennai

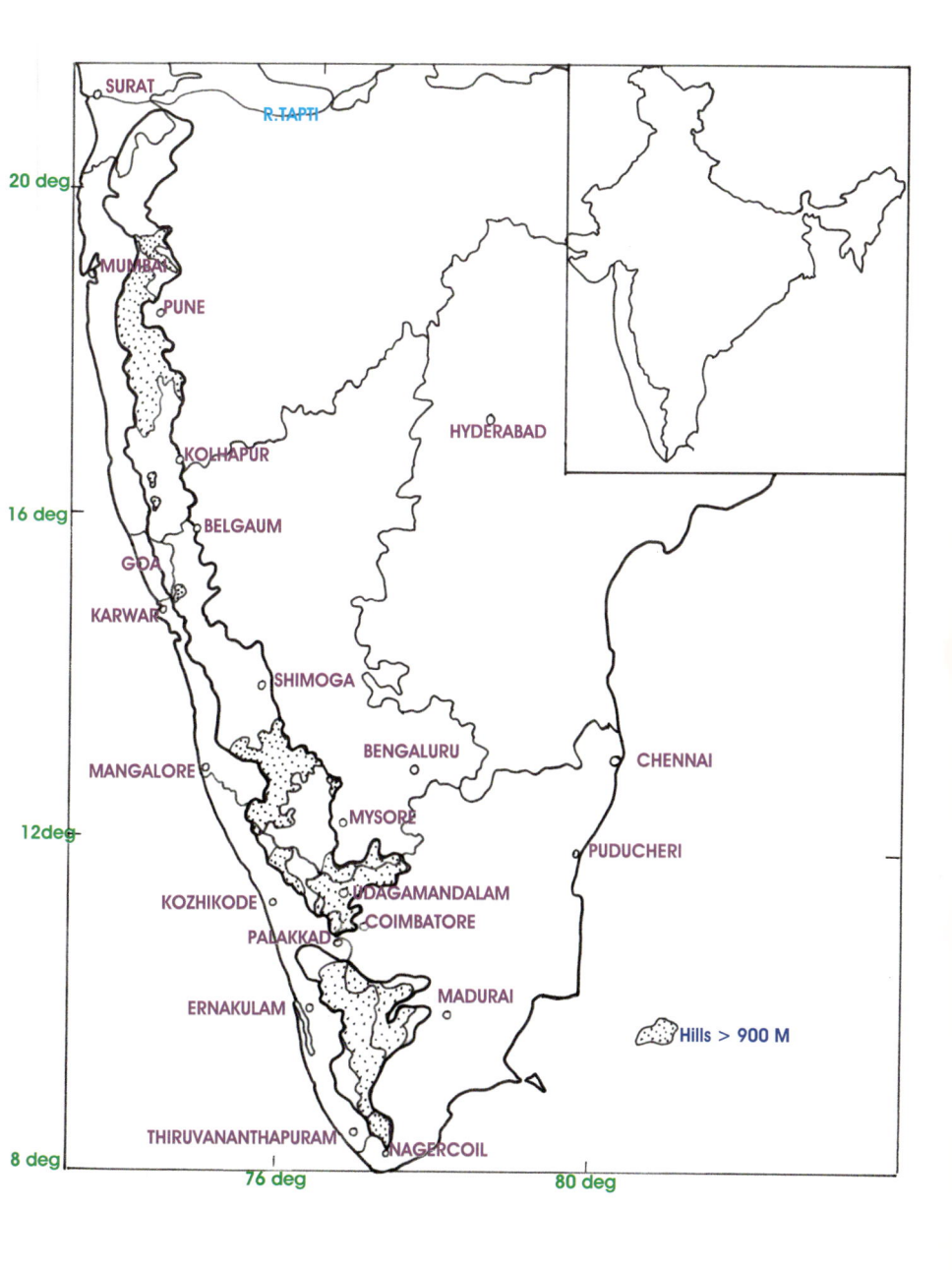

SURAT	
R. TAPTI	
20 deg	
MUMBAI	
PUNE	
KOLHAPUR	
16 deg	
BELGAUM	
GOA	
KARWAR	
SHIMOGA	
HYDERABAD	
MANGALORE	
BENGALURU	
CHENNAI	
12 deg	
MYSORE	
PUDUCHERI	
KOZHIKODE	
UDAGAMANDALAM	
PALAKKAD	COIMBATORE
ERNAKULAM	MADURAI
THIRUVANANTHAPURAM	NAGERCOIL
8 deg	
76 deg	80 deg

Hills > 900 M

Origins

From Gondwanaland to Asia

It's been 150 million years since peninsular India broke away from the massive southern landmass of the Gondwanaland and started drifting northwards. It perhaps collided with mainland Asia nearly a hundred million years later. The landmass was lifted up like a dome during the northward drift over the active Reunion Hotspots—underwater volcanoes that were two hundred–three hundred kilometres wide. And just before peninsular India became part of Asia, the dome cracked along the middle, letting the western half sink below the sea, and giving rise to the Western Ghats.

Major changes in the relief and climate of peninsular India followed this event. Firstly, the entire landmass suffered an eastward tilt, leading to a predominantly easterly drainage. Torrential streams and cascades characterised the western side of the peninsula, changing the courses of rivers permanently. Secondly, there emerged a more seasonal pattern of rainfall, later known as the monsoons, creating distinct climatic zones along the north-south and east-west gradients. A continuous process of weathering eventually moulded the Western Ghats into its present topography about fifteen million years ago, with peaks rising to over 2,000 metres above sea level, the highest being the Anaimudi Peak at 2,695 metres. And in its 1600 kilometre length that spans the Equator and the Tropic of Cancer, it is broken just once by the Palghat gap that is 170-300 metres above sea level and thirty kilometres wide.

Western Ghats is without any doubt one of the oldest hill chains in the world. Although the prehistoric volcanoes that erupted sixty-five million years ago, rendered the northern segment of the hill chain rather different in topography, much of the Western Ghats has retained the original Gondwanaland geology; the rocks along its surface have remained unchanged for

The natural high-elevation grasslands and shola forests restricted to the south

over two billion years. The collision with Asia made peninsular India a melting pot of Eurasian and Gondwanaland biodiversity.

Forty-five million years of Eurasian influence, and the range of new habitats that emerged, favoured the evolution of a great diversity of life in peninsular India. However, the fluctuating climate induced by the Pleistocene ice cover, 1.5 million years ago, and the subsequent increase in temperature and seasonality, drove much of the unique biodiversity that evolved in peninsular India into the Western Ghats, where the mountainous topography and wet conditions have continued to shelter them. This includes some of earth's ancient and relic plants and animals. *(see table 1)*

Endemic plants such as *Rhododendron*, endemic mammals including the Nilgiri Tahr and the Nilgiri Marten, and endemic birds like laughing thrushes, seen today in the Western Ghats, are indeed examples of relic invaders from Eurasia. Other such examples of plants and animals showing a greater affinity to the

Eurasian flora and fauna had guided early naturalists like Sunderlal Hora to overemphasise the northern ancestry of the Western Ghats' biodiversity.

Sunderlal Hora, in his much-acclaimed Satpura Hypothesis, postulated that the endemic hill stream fishes of the Western Ghats were almost entirely derived from 'elsewhere', especially from the Indo-Malayan region. This theory so fascinated biologists for a few decades that the origin and evolution of biodiversity in the Western Ghats were more or less blindly attributed to the supposed 'landbridge' that connected the eastern Himalayas with the northern Western Ghats. Modern research has, however, provided enough evidence to suggest that Sunderlal Hora was quite wrong in his assumptions. That some of Gondwanaland's biodiversity had actually moved north through peninsular India has been substantiated, amongst others, by the distribution pattern of hornworts belonging to the genus *Notothylas* (family Notothylaceae) which have their greatest diversity in the Western Ghats.

These rocks are two billion years old

Plants, invertebrates and the cold-blooded vertebrates, including fish, amphibians, and reptiles, appeared on earth much before birds and mammals did. There is growing evidence that many of the unique species found today in the Western Ghats have had a very ancient history. According to the biotic ferry biogeographic model, they apparently evolved *in situ* during the northward drift of peninsular India. Amongst plants, trees from the Bonnetiaceae family are probably the best examples to illustrate the Gondwanaland connection. Legless amphibians (caecilians) from the Caecilidae family that are found in the tropical parts of America, Africa, Seychelles and Asia, including nine species endemic to the Western Ghats, are other good examples. These amphibians are known to have survived through the past sixty-five million years, that is, at least ten million years before peninsular India became part of Asia.

Unfortunately, due to the paucity of fossil records and DNA-based phylogenetic studies covering a wider range of plants and animals, it has not been possible to precisely trace the prehistory of the endemic families, genera, and species of organisms belonging to the Western Ghats. The diverse family of burrowing shield-tail snakes (Uropeltidae), with relatives only in Sri Lanka; more than ten species of large, carp-like fishes in the genus *Hypselobarbus*, largely confined to the Western Ghats; the endemic wrinkled frogs (*Nyctibatrachus*), torrent frogs *(Micrixalus)*, and leaping frogs (*Indirana*), represented by over twenty species in the Western Ghats—many such examples have raised a number of questions regarding the origin of the biodiversity in the Western Ghats.

The dams and tea gardens have fragmented the rain-forests as seen in the picture

A few recent discoveries of amphibian species in the Western Ghats have shed more light on *in situ* evolution and speciation during the hundred million years when peninsular India was drifting northwards. Specific examples that have supported the biotic ferry model include the fossil frog *Indobatrachus pusillus*. This extinct frog is believed to represent an ancient Indo-Madagascan lineage of amphibians that flourished in peninsular India before it collided with Asia. The recently discovered pig-nosed frog (*Nasikabatrachus sahyadrensis*) is probably the best example to illustrate the Gondwanaland affinity in the biodiversity of the Western Ghats. This frog represents an exclusive family (Nasikabatrachidae) that apparently branched out more than 130 million years ago from the sooglossid frogs found only in Seychelles.

A specimen of the pig-nosed frog was collected by Professor M.I. Andrews about ten years ago, and preserved at the Mar Thoma College in Kottayam. Prof Andrews considered it to be one of the better-known species of balloon frogs (*Uperodon globulosus,* Microhylidae), and, hence, did not realise its biological significance. Thanks to subsequent collections from other parts of Kerala, including the Anaimalai Hills, the biogeographical significance of this unique species of frog has now been brought to light. Interestingly, more examples of Nasikabatrachus collected in recent years have suggested that more than one species belong to this endemic genus of burrowing frogs.

A wind-worn *Rhododendron* tree in the Nilgiri Hills

The pig-nosed frog is just one example; there are many more. It has been estimated that thirty to forty percent of all species that occur in the Western Ghats could be endemic — species that do not naturally occur elsewhere. Where did they come from? How long have they been isolated from their ancestors? Modern biological techniques adopted by taxonomists will, no doubt, aid in a better understanding of the origin and evolutionary history of the biodiversity in Western Ghats.

Table 1: Endemic Species of the Western Ghats

Group	Total species	Endemic species	Endemism
Bryophytes (Mosses and Liverworts)	803	200	25
Flowering plants	4500	1720	38
Butterflies	330	37	11
Dragonflies and damselflies	178	70	39
Fishes	225	123	55
Amphibians	138	110	80
Reptiles	161	99	61
Birds	508	13	< 3
Mammals	120	12	10

Geography

A Landscape Unsurpassed

Rains, clouds and mist have together given the Western Ghats its popular Indian name, *Sahyadris* or the rain hills. This hilly landscape of 160,000 square kilometres receives an average annual rainfall of 250 centimetres. Although rainfall may be as low as one hundred centimetres on the eastern side, local extremes of 1,000 centimetres or more are not uncommon in the Western Ghats. Such wet spots in the Anaimalai Hills, Nilgiri Hills (the Blue Mountains) and Maharashtra have rivalled Agumbe in Karnataka, which is known for its wetness with an annual average of 750 centimetres.

A vivid morning sky over the barren coastal hills

It rains almost all the year round in the southern parts, while areas towards the northern limit remain dry for eight to nine months. The climate is generally tropical—warm and humid, becoming hot in summer and rather cold in winter, especially in the north and in the mountainous south. Temperatures low enough to trigger surface frost is experienced in the Nilgiri Hills and other mountains of comparable elevation. Interestingly, in many parts of the southern Western Ghats the lowest temperatures are encountered during the wettest time of the year, i.e. July and August, and not during winter.

High wind speeds on the mountain tops, torrential rains, temperature fluctuations, and varying spells of dryness in harmony with the local topography and geology, have given rise to a wide variety of natural vegetation types in the Western Ghats. Despite the different ways in which they have been classified from

Irony in the Nilgiri Hills; the western catchment and its garbage-lined access

time to time, all vegetation that occurred naturally in the Western Ghats would belong to one of the two broad types—grasslands and forests. *(see table 2)*

Contrary to the popular notion that the grasslands were originally created as pastures by early humans, it has now been shown that they existed as early as 50,000 years ago. Moreover, some of the present patterns of distribution of the typical grassland species of plants and animals, especially birds like the Nilgiri Pipit, that are endemic to the Western Ghats, have reinforced the scientific view that the high altitude grasslands are indeed natural and quite ancient.

Remarkable amongst the landscape features of the Western Ghats is the limestone outcrop localised in northern Karnataka that is home to rock pigeons and rock bees. The castle-like formation in Yan of Uttara Kannada district is the only one of its kind in the entire Western Ghats. Limestone outcrops of similar nature are more widely distributed and common in South-east Asia.

The complex topography, soil conditions and rainfall have together influenced the structure and species composition of the forests in the Western Ghats. Low-lying, waterlogged areas within evergreen forests have created an ideal habitat for species of wild nutmeg (*Myristica*), wild pepper (*Piper*), and a variety of

Table 2: Major Vegetation Types of the Western Ghats

Broad Category and Vegetation type	Altitude ASL and Rainfall	Dominant plants
Forests Shola characterised by short trees 15–20 m high 2500–5000 mm	Above 1500 m; rainfall	Actinodaphne, Elaeocarpus, Eunymus, Michelia, Rhodomyrtus, Schefflera, Symplocos, etc.
Tropical evergreen forest scharacterised by emergent trees up to 60 m in height	200–1500 m; 2500–5000 mm rainfall	Acrocarpus, Aglaia, Artocarpus, Calophyllum, Canarium, Cullenia, Dipterocarpus, Holigarna, Knema. Myristica, etc.
Moist deciduous forests	500–900 m; 2500–3500 mm rainfall	Bridelia, Pterocarpus, Sterculia, Pterospermum, Lagerstroemia, Tectona, Terminalia, etc.
Dry deciduous forests	300–900 m; 1000–2000 mm rainfall	Albizia, Anogeissus, Bauhinia, Buchanania, Butea, Dillenia, Emblica, etc.
Scrub jungles	200–500 m; 300–600 mm rainfall	Acacia, Carissa, Capparis, Flacourtia, Gardenia, etc.
Grasslands High rainfall savannas	Above 2000 m; > 5000 mm rainfall	Grass, herbs and Shrubs Ligustrum, Rhododendron, Anaphalis, Strobilanthes, etc.
Peat bogs	Above 2000 m; 2500–5000 mm rainfall	Grasses, sedges and mosses – Carex, Cyanotis, Cyperus, Eriocaulon, etc.
Savannas	1700–1900 m; 2500–3500 mm rainfall	Grass Chrysopogon, Arundinella, Eulalia, Heteropogon, etc.

Note: ASL (Above Sea Level)

palms and ferns that grow well under the forest canopy and in waterlogged soil. Many of the trees in these swamps have evolved special roots that look like stilts and knees, similar to those found in mangrove forests. Such swamps, popularly known as the *Myristica* swamps, are found in the Western Ghats southwards from Karnataka.

Besides the *Myristica* swamps, there are rainforest swamps dominated by the endemic palm *Pinanga dicksonii*. More recent research in the Western Ghats of Tirunelveli and Kanyakumari districts has disclosed the presence of a hitherto little-studied swamp community dominated by the *Elaeocarpus* species. Interestingly, these *Elaeocarpus* swamps are found only in the middle and high elevations, and the trees there do not show any obvious physiognomic adaptations. Muthukuzhulivayal in the Western Ghats of Kanyakumari district is dotted with numerous such swamps.

Dams and their footprints, mist-covered hilltops and placid pools characterise the region

WESTERN GHATS | 11

There are many other kinds of rather localised landscape features which are also widely distributed. Patches of vegetation predominantly supporting cane, other palms, and bamboo called brakes characterised the Western Ghats in the recent past. Rock outcrops, cascading waterfalls, and torrential streams have all contributed to the diverse landscape. They have not only made the landscape scenic but also provided specialised niches for a number of rare plants and animals. The spray zone of the Jog Falls, for instance, was once the best habitat for the now locally extinct species of grass *Hubbardia heptaneuron*.

Grasslands in the Mukurti NP where the tahr still roam

Velvety forest canopy, giant trees bursting out their branches into the sky, drifting clouds, mist, and the noise of rushing waters and waves of cicada song have characterised the Western Ghats through the ages. Hundreds of lovely birds and their delightful songs, thousands of frogs that sing at night, herds of elephants and deer, troops of macaques and langur, a chattering giant squirrel, an occasional tiger, and the sudden whiz of a hornbill's wings, bring alive the otherwise still and serene landscape. It is an awesome landscape, unsurpassed indeed in its magnificence and splendour.

Muddy torrents of Magod after the rains

Flora and Fauna
Of Creatures Great and Small

The magnitude of biodiversity in the Western Ghats is not fully known. The range of variations that some species demonstrate, together with the diverse stages of life history that many others have evolved, add to the great diversity of life. The magnitude of biodiversity is, however, most readily assessed by using species—biological populations that naturally interbreed as the unit. An educated guess might place the number of species in this biogeographical province between 10,000 and 15,000. These species include tiny single-celled organisms like bacteria, amoeba and a range of parasites, and the more complex multi-celled fungi, plants and animals, some growing into giants like the fifty-metre-high *Tetrameles nudis* trees, and, of course, the elephants.

Wild raspberries (*Rubus*) were probably carried by birds during the ice ages

The humid climatic conditions prevailing round the year in most of these parts, except the highest hills, provide the most suitable environment for hundreds of microscopic organisms. These minute organisms are everywhere, although invisible to the naked eye. They are in the soil, water, and decomposing matter; on leaves, branches and tree trunks; amongst hair on mammals; between feathers on birds and scales on reptiles; on the skin of amphibians; on fishes and insects; and within most living plants and animals as parasites or through symbiotic associations.

Micro-organisms manifest their presence most commonly through odour and colour. Many of the unusual odours felt, while walking through the forests and hillsides in the Western Ghats, are those produced by these organisms. Unusual colours of soil, and of rock surfaces, bark and leaves, as well as water, may all be manifestations of millions of micro-organisms. Unfortunately, due to a number of constraints, including the difficulties in identifying species of micro-organisms, there is little agreement among biologists on the magnitude of their diversity in the Western Ghats.

Rusts, Mildew and Mushrooms

Fungi are not strictly considered to be micro-organisms. They tend to exist both in microscopic and macro-forms. Modern biologists treat all fungi as representatives of an exclusive kingdom of living organisms called 'fungia'. The most common fungus that occurs throughout the Western Ghats is *Polyporus* (family Polyporaceae). The dry, brown and bracket-like bodies with a distinct stalk that grow on dead branches belong to this group.

Many fungi, including *Polyporus*, after passing through the microscopic spore and mycelium stages, produce conspicuous reproductive parts. Fungi that produce conspicuous, fleshy reproductive organs are commonly known as mushrooms. Of the six hundred species of known fungi from the Western Ghats, four hundred are mushrooms. Some species of mushroom are extremely toxic while many others are edible.

The common wood-rotting fungus (*Polyporus*)

Microscopic fungi can cause plant and animal diseases. The common rusty spots and white powdery mildew seen on leaves are symptoms of fungal diseases in plants. Cultivation and plantation

Mushrooms like this go unnoticed amidst the vivid colours of the naturalised *Helichrysum, Asclepias and Jacaranda*

The mist adapted *Anaphalis*

16 | WESTERN GHATS

activitities have created conditions favourable for the proliferation of these pathogenic fungi which destroy plants. Pathogenic fungi belonging to the genera *Aspergillus* and *Fusarium* are known to be in abundance in the Western Ghats.

Non-parasitic mildew that grows on leaf surfaces is yet another group of microscopic fungi that has attracted biologists. Black or dark mildews, which make leaves look as if coated with soot, belong to the family Meliolaceae. Nearly 487 varieties of these mildews are known to exist in the Western Ghats. At least 398 species belong to just one genus, viz., *Meliola*.

Soils in the Western Ghats are full of fungi. Some soil fungi are free-living, while others live in association with trees. Fungi that live around the roots are called ectomycorhiza while those living within the roots are known as arbuscular mycorhiza. These fungi help trees in absorbing soil nutrients for better growth and survival. Some of the common ectomycorhiza that have been isolated from the soils in the Western Ghats are *Pisolithus, Scleroderma* and *Ramaria*. Common arbuscular mycorhizae are known to belong to the genera *Glomus, Gigasporia, Scutellospora, Acaulospora* and *Sclerocystis*.

Plants

At least 6,750 species of plants from the Western Ghats are already known to us. These include around three hundred species of algae, eight hundred species of lichens (which, strictly speaking, belong to the class of fungi), 850 species of bryophytes (liverworts, hornworts and mosses), three hundred species of ferns and allies (pteridophytes), and 4,500 species of flowering plants. Botanists believe that there are many more species of algae, lichens and bryophytes in the Western Ghats that have not yet been discovered.

The most common algae in Western Ghats are probably the green algae that belong to the family chlorophyceae. These algae grow on the surfaces of submerged rocks in shallow and fast flowing streams, and make 'rock-hopping' a risky business! Lichens, unlike algae, are not aquatic. Although they have evolved from algae in association with fungi, they occur outside water on leaves, barks and rocks. They are not only graceful in form but also spectacular in colour.

Leaf-like (foliose) lichens are widespread in the Western Ghats. Foliose lichens in the genus *Parmelina* are apparently the most diverse. There are ninety species of *Parmelina* in the Western Ghats. Higher up in the mountains, the landscape is so full of lichens that it makes rocks and tree trunks glitter. One common genus of lichen that grows on branches along the roadsides in the higher elevations is Usnea. Due to their lanky appearance, these lichens are popularly called the old man's beard.

Species of *Ceropegia* are amongst the most endangered of Indian plants

The Western Ghats are home to a diverse flora of bryophytes with around two hundred endemic species. *(see table 1)* Experts at the Botanical Survey of India have listed around 170 species from the Wayanad district in Kerala. Further south in the Kanyakumari district of Tamil Nadu, 191 species that represent forty-five families and seventy-five genera have been identified. Among these are 117 species of mosses, seventy-three of liverworts, and three species of hornworts. A few new species have also been added to the already existing list of species.

Among more than 850 known species of bryophytes, only 140 are liverworts and hornworts. The families Chonecoleaceae and Schistochilaceae are endemic to the region. The family with the largest number of species is, however, Lejeuneaceae, in which there are twenty-three species in the genus *Cololejeunea* alone. *Heteroscyphus* and *Lophocolea* (family Geocalcyaceae) are the most widespread genera of liverworts in Western Ghats.

Ixoras are amongst the few native plants that have found a place in domestic gardens

Other known genera of liverworts include *Anthoceros, Dumortiera, Frullania, Lunularia, Roboulia* and *Schistochila*. Amongst hornworts, Notothylas has diversified the most in the Western Ghats.

Bryophytes in Western Ghats are predominantly mosses, with nearly 682 known species. Among these, 190 are endemic, mostly belonging to the Pottiaceae and Bryaceae families. The genus *Fissidens* is the most widespread in the Western Ghats.

Handeliobyrum setschwanicum, a species of moss discovered in the Silent Valley around thirty years ago, was earlier known to exist only in northeast India and China. Similarly, *Fissidens griffithii* that has been recently found in the Kanyakumari district was earlier considered endemic to Bhutan.

Amongst the non-flowering plants, ferns and allied plants (pteridophytes) are probably the most diverse in size and shape. Though many are small and herbaceous in nature, tree ferns in the genus *Cyathea* grow into giants resembling palms. Tree ferns are also rather ancient and have survived through the prehistoric geological ages. They inhabit hills in the higher elevations and narrow streamlets in dark ravines. Another common giant fern that shares the habitat of the tree fern in the Western Ghats is *Angiopteris erecta*. Including the handful of aquatic (*Acrostichum aureum, Marselia minuta, Salvinia molesta*) and epiphytic ferns (*Drynaria quercifolia*), there are 320 known species in the Western Ghats.

The southern Western Ghats are richer in pteridophytes than the northern half. Approximately three-fourths (239 species) of the pteridophytes are known to flourish south of the Palghat Gap alone. The most important habitats for ferns and allied plants are banks of streams in evergreen forests and the *shola*. Pteridophyte diversity is highest at altitudes of eight hundred metres and more above the sea level (ASL). Ferns that are diverse in the south are *Asplenium* (twenty-two species), *Pteris* (eleven species), *Adiantum* (ten species), and *Cyathea* (three species). *Pteridium aquilinum* is the common bracken (fern) found throughout the mountainous habitats in Western Ghats. A dense growth of this common (and fire resistant) invasive fern can be seen along the steep slopes of the Nilgiri Hills (bordering grasslands) and other moist hill ranges. Some of the common fern allies in the southern landscapes are *Lycopodiella cernua, Selaginella involvens, Selaginella intermedia, Selaginella delicatula* and *Selaginella tenera*.

Centella asiatica—a common medicinal plant

There are 4,500 species of flowering plants in the Western Ghats, including a few gymnosperms—naked seeded plants. Two species of cycads (family Cycadaceae), *Cycas circinalis* and *Cycas annaikalii*; one conifer *Nageia* (*Podocarpus*) *wallichiana*; and two species of gnetales, *Gnetum ula* and *Gnetum contractum,* comprise the native gymnosperm flora. The rest are angiosperms—flowering plants in which the seeds are enclosed in a fruit. In all, there are around two hundred known families of flowering plants in the Western Ghats, represented by 1,300-1,400 genera. These include fifty-four endemic genera, including forty-two monotypic ones—genera that are known by a single species each.

The diversity of flowering plants in the Western Ghats is mainly due to the shrubs, herbs, and grasses. four hundred species of grasses (family Poaceae), classified under 120 genera, largely contribute to this diversity. These include many species of bamboos, especially the climbing bamboo found in the rainforests of the Meghamalai Hills. The large and diverse beans family (Leguminosae) comes next, with more than 320 species, represented by eighty-five genera.

Blue-black berries tend to attract fruit-eating birds

Interestingly, other families represented by a large number of species, except the families Euphorbiaceae and Rubiaceae, are those that generally lack woody plants growing more than ten metres high. These highly diverse families include orchidaceae (orchids; sixty genera and 250 species); acanthaceae (crossandra-like herbs and shrubs; forty-five genera and 165 species); cyperaceae (sedges; twenty-one genera and 160 species); euphorbiaceae (latex-producing plants related to rubber and poinsettia; fifty-five genera and 140 species); asteraceae (asters and allies; fifty-seven genera and 130 species; species of *Vernonia* may grow to be trees higher than ten metres); lamiaceae (plants related to *tulasi*; twenty-five genera and 115 species); rubiaceae (plants related to coffee; forty genera and hundred species); and asclepiadaceae (milkweed and allied plants; thirty genera and ninety species).

Although trees determine the nature of forests and different habitats in most terrestrial ecosystems throughout the world, they are not as diverse in species as are shrubs, herbs, and grasses. Despite their conspicuousness, only one out of every six species of flowering plants in the Western Ghats may be a tree. More than sixty percent of all families of flowering plants in the Western Ghats do not grow into trees. There are 650 species of trees here, representing a little over 320 genera and sixty-eight families.

Non-native conifers have become a part of the hills in the south

Not less than 1,720 species of flowering plants are endemic to the Western Ghats. Half the number of the orchid species found here are endemic. Around 350 species of endemic plants are trees. In other words, trees contribute to less than one-fourth of the endemic flowering plant diversity. The tree genus with the largest number of endemic species is *Syzigium*. Twenty endemic species in the Western Ghats belong to this genus of plants, closely related to the *jamun,* rose apple, and clove. Two other genera of trees have more than ten endemic species—the *Diospyros* (fourteen species) and the *Cinnamomum* (thirteen species). The former is the genus to which the African ebony belongs, and the latter genus of trees has provided us the widely used spice, cinnamon.

Some species of trees that are found in the Western Ghats have had a rather ancient lineage. One of the relic genera of trees that have Gondwanaland affinity is *Poeciloneuron* that belongs to the family Bonnetiaceae. The two species, *Poeciloneuron indicum* and *Poeciloneuron pauciflorum,* endemic to the southern forests have their nearest relatives in South America. Other examples of ancient trees may belong to genera *Pittosporum* (family Pittosporaceae), *Gomphandra, Apodytes, Nothapodytes* (family Icacinaceae), and *Hydnocarpus* (family Flacourtiaceae).

A handful of endemic trees found in elevations higher than 1,500 metres are Eurasian in origin. Their nearest relatives are found only in the Himalayas. Well-known examples of trees with a northern affinity are *Rhododendron arboreum* (family Ericaceae), *Rhodomyrtus tomentosa* (family Myrtaceae) and *Mahonia leschenaultii* (family Beriberidaceae).

A ground orchid

A stony brook

Many species of flowering plants in the Western Ghats are rare and, therefore, considered endangered. According to some botanists, 410 species of flowering plants are endangered, including 235 endemic species. Low population size, small geographical ranges, and specialised habitat requirements are major factors that contribute to the rarity and the threat of extinction of flowering plants in the Western Ghats.

Insects

Animals constitute the major part of the biodiversity in Western Ghats. This tremendous diversity is mainly due to the invertebrates, especially insects, whose diversity in tropical regions surpasses that of plants and vertebrate animals. This is a global phenomenon that holds true in the Western Ghats too. In fact, some estimates have suggested that up to sixty percent of all species could be insects. Considering the conservative estimate of 10,000–15,000 species for the Western Ghats, a simple calculation suggests that there could be at least 6,000 insect species in the region. The richness of species would be much more if we added the other invertebrates to this list.

A graceful damselfly (*Vestalis gracilis*)

An untrained eye does not even see the enormous diversity of invertebrates—animals without backbones, including all those 'creepy, crawly, fearsome creatures' that an average citizen unfortunately resents—that a region like the Western Ghats might boast of, leave alone being able to identify even one percent of the species. For example, during the expedition to Silent Valley in 1979, amongst others there were botanists and zoologists in the team. One version of the report of the expedition that got published many years later, lists out important groups of animals that were collected, including Nematahelminthes, Annelida, Crustacea, Collembola, Diplura, Thysanura, Odonata,

The Indian laburnum

Orthoptera, Phasmida, Dermaptera, Isoptera, Hemiptera, Thysanoptera, Neuroptera, Lepidoptera, Diptera, Dictyoptera, Hymenoptera, Coleoptera, Arachnida, Myriapoda and Mollusca. These groups pertain to invertebrate animals, and include round worms, earthworms, crabs and prawns, snails, spiders, scorpions, millipedes, centipedes, and a variety of insects such as springtails, double-tails, silver fish, dragonflies, damselflies, grasshoppers, crickets, stick insects, leaf insects, earwigs, termites, bugs, cicadas, thrips, ant lions, lace wings, butterflies, moths, flies, praying mantises, cockroaches, ants, wasps, beetles and weevils!

Tea gardens have fragmented the southern landscape much more than all other land uses

Exhaustive, to say the least, but what do we know of the diversity in each of these groups of invertebrate animals? Of course, as in most parts of the world, butterflies are the best studied insects in Western Ghats. There are 330 species of butterflies representing 166 genera and five families. While there could be an elusive brown or a skipper that is not yet known, chances of adding many more species to the existing list of butterflies is rather bleak. Although there are only thirty-seven species of butterflies that are endemic, they have had rather diverse origins and evolutionary histories. The small butterfly *Colias nilgiriensis* (family Pieridae), found in the mountainous parts of Kerala and Tamil Nadu, for instance, is a Eurasian relic.

The 330 species of butterflies depend on over a thousand species of flowering plants for their survival. In other words, one out of every four species of flowering plants in the Western Ghats is food to the caterpillar of at least one species of butterfly. Many species apparently depend exclusively on certain species of plants. Reliance on a single species of plant as larval food has been so rigid in certain species of butterflies that the presence of the host plant has been accurately predicted in a number of instances merely by the presence of the butterfly in a locality.

Butterflies of the Western Ghats sport a diversity of sizes, shapes and colours. The largest species is the Southern birdwing that has a wingspan of nineteen centimetres; a measure comparable to the span of the hand of an adult human. The bright yellow and black wing pattern renders the species spectacular. Another large butterfly, though not showy, is the Malabar tree nymph that has a wingspan of sixteen centimetres. With the exception of the tree nymph (family Nymphalidae), butterflies with a wingspan of around ten centimetres are all swallowtails (family Papilionidae). Blue mormon, red Helen and Paris peacock are the most spectacular swallowtails in the region.

A native *Memecylon* in full bllom

The majority of the butterfly species in the Western Ghats are smaller, with wingspans not more than five centimetres, and rather plain or drab coloured. The smallest is probably the grass jewel (family Lycaenidae) with a wingspan of 1.5–2 centimetres. These are the butterflies that the untrained eye normally misses as the insects sit motionless on dry leaves or within grass. The evening browns or satyrs (family Nymphalidae) and skippers (family Hesperiidae) are often mistaken for moths due to their drab colouration and habit of flying at dusk. That most butterflies are day-fliers has made them ecologically different from the moths.

Butterflies and moths belong to the same order of insects known as lepidoptera—meaning scaly-winged insects. There are many more species of moths than there are butterflies, making it difficult for anyone to guess the possible diversity of moths in the Western Ghats. Moths also show a greater range of variation in their size. Some are so small, measuring less than half a centimetre across spread wings, that they are classified as 'micro-lepidoptera'. Insects that are popularly known as 'leaf-miners', belong to this group of moths. They are the ones that produce the silvery snake-like streaks on the surface of leaves. These mines shelter the larvae as they feed and grow.

A sample of the hundreds of naturalised ornamental plants

The largest moths include the Atlas moths, wild silk moths, lunar moths (family Saturnidae), and owlet moths (family Noctuidae). Atlas moths (*Attacus*) may have wingspans exceeding fifteen centimetres; the largest species in the genus *Attacus atlas* has a wingspan of thirty centimetres. The Indian lunar or moon moth, *Actias selene* has a wingspan of twelve centimetres. Since moths in general have much heavier wings and abdomen than

WESTERN GHATS

These ornamentals have been introduced from Alpine meadows

Rauvolfia serpentina, a rare native

butterflies, they normally weigh much more than butterflies of comparable wingspans. Similarly, moth larvae (caterpillars) can grow to be much larger and heavier than butterfly larvae. In the Western Ghats, more often the large and spectacular moth caterpillars—some sporting large eye-spots or antler-like stinging armour and exceeding ten centimetres in length—are the best telltale signs of the presence of huge moths in the locality. Their large size, tendency to congregate in big numbers, and enormous appetites, render moth caterpillars more devastating in nature. Thus, many species prove to be pests of forest trees, especially those in monoculture plantations.

After butterflies, probably the best-known group of insects are ants, with 350 known species found in the Western Ghats. Ants are closely related to wasps and honey bees. Many species are equipped with powerful stings. In fact, the red-and-black tree ant (*Tetraponera rufonigra*), that is very common in the Western Ghats, is known to deliver the most painful of stings amongst ants. Most other species of the stinging ants are ground dwelling. Species of ants in the genus *Crematogaster* build nests on trees that crudely resemble the paper wasp's nest. The rufous woodpeckers often excavate hollows in these ant nests and brood eggs. Interestingly, the ants also use surrogate nests. They make tiny holes on the egg capsules of praying mantises and share the space with the developing young mantises.

The largest ant is the forest floor ant *Camponotus*

angusticollis. Worker ants of this species can measure as much as two centimetres. Other large forest floor ants include *Bothroponera ruficeps* (1.8 centimetres) and *Harpegnathos saltator* (1.6 centimetres). The latter, commonly known as the jumping ant, has the ability to leap like spiders. It also drags paralysed spiders between its legs like wasps.

Many species of forest floor ants as well as those that live on trees tend to be very small in size; the workers do not exceed 0.3 centimetre in length. The smallest worker ants, smaller than 0.1 centimetre in length, may be found in the genus Solenopsis. Others of comparable size may be found in the genera *Monomorium, Pheidole, Tetramorium, Bothriomyrmex, Tapinoma* and *Plagiolepis.* The smallest species in these genera have worker ants that do not exceed 0.2 centimetre in length whereas the larger species of ants are largely predatory and carrion eating; the smallest ants feed on nectar, flowers and seeds.

Amongst the other groups of insects that are fairly well-known in Western Ghats are the dragonflies and damselflies (order Odonata). A total of 178 species in thirteen families are known, of which seventy are endemic. The single largest family is

One of the many showy damselflies (*Euphaea cardinalis*)

Photo: K A Subramanian

A common dragonfly *(Ictinogomphus rapax)*

Photo: K A Subramanian

Libellulidae (dragonflies) with over fifty species. Other families with a large number of species are Gomphidae (twenty-seven species), Coenagrionidae (twenty-five species) and Cordulidae (twenty species). The family Platycenemididae is the smallest with just one genus *Copera* represented by two species.

Seventy-four percent of all the endemic species of odonates are represented by just four families—Gomphidae (eighteen species), Cordulidae (sixteen species), Protoneuridae (eleven species), and Platystictidae (seven species). All but one species in the family Platystictidae are endemic. Interestingly, the family Libellulidae with the largest number of species has just two species that are endemic to the Western Ghats.

The largest dragonflies are found in the family Aeschnidae. The larger species may have a body length of over ten centimetres and a wingspan close to fifteen centimetres. These fast-flying species are hard to notice, despite their large size, unless they are at rest. The most spectacularly coloured members of the order Odonata are nevertheless the damselflies. Damselflies are easily identified by their slender abdomens, hammer-like heads, and brightly coloured wings that are closed above the body when at rest. A brief visit to any stream in the Western Ghats offers the best treat of damselflies to the human eye.

Of the thirteen families of Odonata, eight are treated as damselflies. There are sixty-eight known species of damselflies in the region. Although damselflies are represented by a larger number of families, there are more species of dragonflies in the

Western Ghats. However, if the proportion of endemic species is considered in relation to the total number of species in each group, damselflies fare better than dragonflies. Forty-five percent of all damselflies are endemic to the Western Ghats whereas only thirty-five percent of the dragonflies are endemic.

All species in the order Odonata have aquatic nymphs. Nymphs are predators which feed on smaller aquatic invertebrates, sometimes little fish and tadpoles. Adult damselflies and dragonflies are both predators. Hence, they are considered to be potential agents in the biological control of insect pests. Further, the nymphs, being sensitive to biophysical changes in water, have been identified as candidates useful in bio-monitoring aquatic ecosystems.

Streams in the Western Ghats are home to a large number of insects. Some insects use aquatic habitats only during their larval stages whereas many others, including certain beetles and bugs, spend all their life in water. These insects belong to thirteen orders—fifty-three families and eighty genera. Interestingly, recent studies have disclosed the presence of mayflies of the family Isonychidae (order Ephemeroptera), and net-winged midges of the family Blephariceridae (order Diptera). These insects were earlier known to exist only in the cold waters of the Himalayan and Eurasian streams.

Tropical forests are rich in beetles. Beetles belong to the order Coleoptera, the order of insects with the maximum number of species in the world. There is a great diversity of beetles in the Western Ghats too. This enormous diversity has unfortunately not even been partly documented. Some of the beetles are really big.

A well-tamed tea garden landscape

The largest is perhaps, *Acanthophorus serraticornis*, a long-horned beetle (family Cerambicidae). Adults of the species may exceed ten centimetres in length. Other large beetles belong to the family Lucanidae. Commonly called stag beetles, due to the long antler-like mandibles that the males sport, these beetles can reach lengths of over seven centimetres. *Cladognathus* may reach a length of nine centimetres.

A magnificent male stag beetle

What is amazing about beetles is the great range of size that is demonstrated within a family. Dung beetles (family Scarabeidae) are among the better-known of the lot, considered sacred by the Egyptians. These beetles are known for their habit of rolling pieces of dung on open ground. The dung-balls serve as food for the developing larvae. The dung beetles vary greatly in size. Observation of a small collection of dung beetles from the BRT Hills in Karnataka, displayed at Ashoka Trust for Research in Ecology and the Environment, Bangalore, made it evident that the largest species may well be over a thousand times bigger than the smallest.

Rivalling the diversity of size and shape in beetles are the range of their colours. Jewel beetles (family Buprestidae) and chafers from the family Cetonidae are amongst the most strikingly coloured medium-sized insects. The diversity of size and shapes are reflected in the larval stages as well. The largest grubs (larvae) are those belonging to the family Cerambicidae. These are woodborers and reach lengths of ten to fifteen centimetres. The absence of legs, the large brownish head region and overall creamy white body identify grubs of the long-horned beetles. It is not uncommon to see a handful of well-fed grubs wriggle out of the branches and trunks as forest trees are felled!

Another large grub commonly seen is that of the rhinoceros beetle (*Oryctes rhinoceros*; family Scarabeidae). These white grubs with legs have a brown head and a grey behind. They may grow to around ten centimetres in length and look big. Unlike the grubs of long-horned beetles, rhinoceros beetle grubs grow underground within composting leaf and manure.

Diversity of species in many other groups of insects in Western Ghats has been identified to a certain degree. Grasshoppers, praying mantises, paper wasps, fig wasps, white flies, tingiid bugs, reduviid bugs, gall midges, termites and cicadas have attracted considerable attention. For instance, experts suggest that assassin bugs (reduviidae) in the subfamilies harpoctinae and reduviinae could be the most diverse in Western Ghats.

Termites (white ants; order Isoptera) have attracted much attention as pests that affect timber trees and crops. While many species are ground dwelling, some build extraordinary mounds or foraging tunnels on tree trunks or even mud nests on tall trees. What has, however, been ignored is the collective role of termites as keystone species—species that offer natural services disproportionately more than their actual biomass in any ecosystem.

Termites do certainly qualify as keystone species. They are food to a range of

One of the limestone pinnacles at Yan

animals starting with ants (*Leptogenys* ants specialise in raiding termite colonies), frogs and toads, lizards, birds, and mammals, including human beings. Swarming termites even attract larger birds of prey like the crested honey buzzard. Headlights of a vehicle that attracts swarms of flying termites soon invite scores of toads and geckoes at night. Termites are no doubt the 'krills of the forests and grasslands.'

Besides being food, termites serve the ecosystem by breaking down soil and organic matter. Most importantly, the huge mounds provide air-conditioned shelter for spiders, scorpions, toads, snakes, monitor lizards and even smaller mammals. Within deciduous forests, peacocks and langurs use the tall mounds as watch-towers. Mammals including elephants enjoy rubbing their backs on the hard mounds. There are certainly more species of termites in the Western Ghats than there are fig trees.

No discussion on the insects of the Western Ghats can end without a tribute to the cicadas. These are bugs (order Hemiptera), the only bugs that produce audible sounds. The forests and hillsides reverberate with the songs of millions of cicadas during summer days. The intensity of the sound can be so high that even birds tend to desert areas of the forests where the cicadas lustily sing. The song of the cicada is so

A bronze skink

Elephants wading through invasive *Eupatorium* in Mudumalai

34 | WESTERN GHATS

characteristic that the absence of it during the usual season makes one wonder if all is well. In fact, the well-known landscape of Silent Valley got its name due to the apparent paucity of cicadas. Although there are cicadas in Silent Valley, for some reason that has not yet been understood, they are much fewer in number here than in most other parts of Western Ghats.

Arthropods other than Insects

Other invertebrate animals with jointed legs (arthropods) that we find in the Western Ghats include spiders, scorpions, millipedes, centipedes, wood louse, crabs, and prawns. Most arthropods are land dwelling, except crabs, prawns, shrimps, and other smaller aquatic crustaceans. Interestingly, even the largely marine group of crustaceans known as ostracods are found in the waters of the Western Ghats. These tiny barnacle-like organisms are probably amongst the least known crustaceans in the region.

Of the non-insect arthropods, the spiders are the best known. Spiders, scorpions, and their allies, including the parasitic ticks and mites, are classified together as arachnids. Although the number of scorpion species may be relatively fewer, the approximate number of species of spiders, ticks and mites that the Western Ghats hosts would keep anyone guessing.

Largest of the arachnids are the scorpions. The common large-sized scorpions are those belonging to the family Buthidae and Scorpionidae. Species belonging to the latter are the largest, reaching a total length (trunk and 'tail' together) of fifteen centimetres. The large scorpions that often stray closer to roads and footpaths may belong to either of these families, especially the latter. Related to scorpions are others such as the tiny pseudoscorpions that forage amongst debris and rotting wood, and the whip scorpions. The latter species that are rather big in size live under stones and within rock crevices. *Thelyphonus* has a thin tail, without a sting. The tail-less whip scorpions are more diverse. They lack the whip-like tail, but possess a long flagellum, resembling the antenna of the common cockroach, on each of the first pair of legs. This unusual structure and the overall flattened body, resembling a spider more than a scorpion, readily identify the tail-less whip scorpions.

A short walk through the forests during the dry months is adequate for anyone to get a feeling of the diversity of ticks and mites. But there are other arachnids that are totally harmless. These are the commonly seen long-legged spider-like organisms called harvestmen. Harvestmen stay together in colonies at the base of tree trunks, under overhanging rocks, inside caves, and, sometimes, within dark buildings. They comprise a very diverse, but little-known, group of arachnids.

Spiders are never missed; at least when a web comes in the way. There are 1,442 species of spiders representing fifty-nine families in India. They are everywhere—in all sizes, shapes and colours. According to experts, more than 200 species are known from Western Ghats. And even within smaller landscapes such as the Anaimalai Hills, no less than twenty-seven families of spiders have been reported.

The giant wood spider

Photo: K A Subramanian

Spiders are broadly classified as web spinners and hunters. Web-spinning spiders in the family Araenidae (or Argiopidae) are the most diverse in Western Ghats. Other dominant groups are the jumping spiders (family Salticidae) and the crab spiders (family Thomisidae). Jumping spiders and crab spiders are treated together as 'hunters'. These spiders, which hunt and do not use webs to trap prey, represent more than fifteen families.

The large green cicada—the loudest of all

The largest of the web spinners is the giant wood spider (*Nephila;* family Araneidae). *Nephila malabarensis* is a large and brightly-coloured wood spider that weaves a spectacular web, commonly

Seedlings on a forest floor

seen in almost all forest clearings in the Western Ghats. The web of this species is so strong that even small birds get trapped in it.

Jumping spiders and wolf spiders (family Lycosidae) are commonly seen on low bushes and forest floors. Jumping spiders in the genus *Myrmarachne* are excellent mimics of ants. It is interesting to see a great diversity of these ant-mimicking spiders march alongside armies of ants.

Other common spiders in the Western Ghats include those found on rocks. These spiders belong to the genus *Selenops* (family Selenopidae) and are easily identified by their flattened bodies. *Ctenus* (family Ctenidae) is another fairly large species of forest floor spiders that hunt at night. These spiders are identified by the cat-like markings on their bodies. Then there are the nursery-web weaving or fish-eating spiders (family Pisauridae) that carry the egg sacs under their bodies and stay close to water where they even prey on small fish.

The forests of the Western Ghats are home to a number of species of tarantulas. Tarantulas, sometimes known as 'cat-leg spiders', are really the giants of the spider world. They do not hesitate to enter homes and have often aroused fear amongst local humans. Very little is known about their diversity and habits. Most species of tarantulas in the region belong to the family Theraphosidae. Some of the species in the family are capable of producing hissing sounds when agitated. *Ischnocolus, Poecilotheria, Plesiophrictus, Haploclastus,* and *Ornithoctonus* are some genera of tarantulas in the Western Ghats. *Ornithoctonus gadgili* has been named after Professor Madhav Gadgil who collected it during one of his field trips. Tarantulas in the family Dipluridae possess a pair of long spinnerets that extend beyond the abdomen.

Dillenia pentagyna in full bloom

These spiders build funnel-webs within burrows. Silk-lined burrows of tarantulas are a familiar sight inside the forests, particularly along earth banks and lower cliffs.

Lesser known amongst the non-insect invertebrates with jointed legs are the millipedes and centipedes (class Myriapoda). Millipedes are particularly conspicuous on the forest floors throughout the region. They display a diversity of sizes, shapes, and colours. Giant millipedes may reach lengths well over twenty centimetres. There are many other smaller species. The most interesting of millipedes are the small, pill millipedes

(*Sphaerarthera*) that roll into balls when disturbed. Then they look like seeds on the forest floor, sporting a wide range of colours.

Millipedes feed on fallen fruits and decomposing vegetable matter whereas centipedes are predators. Depending on the size, centipedes feed on anything ranging from termites to small frogs. Most species carry poison in their mandibles, which in the larger species can be potentially dangerous to even human beings. Two families of centipedes are known in India—Cryptopidae (blind centipedes) and Scolopendridae. One hundred species representing eleven genera comprise the Indian centipede fauna.

In the Western Ghats, there is apparently a greater diversity of centipedes than millipedes. Twenty-three species belonging to the family Scolopendridae are known in the state of Kerala alone. These species represent eight genera (*Arthrorhabdus*: one species; *Cormocephalus:* two species; *Scolopendra*: four species; *Asananda*: three species; *Otostigmus*: two species; *Ethmostigmus*: two species; *Digitipes*: five species; *Rhysid*a: four species). The many other species that are known in the region include thin, thread-like soil inhabiting species that are devoid of pigments and perhaps eyes as well, and the many larger species that live under stones and within hollows in trees. Centipedes in the genus *Cormocephalus* are apparently common in India. However, the real giants belong to the genus Scolopendra. The largest species, the tiger centipede (*Scolopendra hardwickei*) may grow to be nearly twenty centimetres in length. These are active hunters that search and overpower small, soft-bodied animals.

Snails, Leeches and Worms

Snails, earthworms, leeches, flatworms, and roundworms are some of the visible groups of invertebrates that have no legs. Snails and slugs are the ones most often seen as they feed and move on tree trunks, rock surfaces and walls. These slow animals, besides the many species of aquatic bivalves (mussels and clams), represent molluscs in the Western Ghats.

The greatest mollusc diversity is in the sea. While most of the Indian species of marine molluscs are known, land and freshwater species, especially those in the Western Ghats, are still not fully known. The largest freshwater snail in India is the apple snail that is represented by the species *Pila virens* in south India. *Pila virens* is common in all ponds and tanks in the lower elevations and foothills. There are many other species of aquatic snails that inhabit even the torrential streams. The most common bivalves belong to the genus *Lamellidens*. Like the apple snail, bivalves are also restricted to the lower elevations.

Very little is known of the diversity of land snails. Recent estimates suggest that even in small landscapes such as Silent Valley, there could be over a hundred species. Elsewhere in the Dakshina Kannada district of Karnataka, fifteen species of land snails have been collected from the Pillarkan sacred grove covering 1.2 square kilometres. These include seven species that are endemic

A colourful land snail gleaning the bark

Photo: K A Subramanian

Biting flies

A giant millipede

to the Western Ghats. *Nicida liricincta* (family Diplommantidae), an endemic species, was the most abundant one, accounting for around forty percent of all the snails that were collected.

Land snails vary in size from the tiny, soil-dwelling species to a few, fairly big, garden snails. In fact, the minute sizes of many species have at least partly been responsible for land snails being elusive. There is no species of land snail in the region that is really large, with a shell dimension that exceeds three to five centimetres, except the introduced giant African snail (*Achatina fulica*) that is locally common. The giant African snail has a tapering shell (resembling the marine Babylonia) that may reach ten centimetres in length.

A variety of worm-like invertebrates are grouped together as helminths. Many are parasitic, spending most of their life inside the guts of mammals, birds, reptiles, and amphibians. Species of microscopic roundworms (Nematodes) live as plant parasites. There could be a large number of such plant parasites in the Western Ghats. Unfortunately, except those that attack crops, the others are poorly known.

Earthworms and leeches in the Western Ghats are also poorly studied. Leeches range in size from the tiny aquatic ones, which are parasitic on fishes and frogs, to the giant horseleech—the large black species with a yellow band along the sides. The horseleech exceeds ten centimetres in length. Land leeches in the Western

Ghats rarely exceed five centimetres in length. While most of them inhabit wet ground, there are some that live in the canopy of trees as well. Although resented by humans, leeches are some of the best indicators of the ecological health of tropical forests.

Around 500 species of earthworms, comprising over sixty genera, are known in India. A few others have been imported for vermi-composting. *Eudrilus eugeniae* (family Eudrilidae) is one common exotic earthworm that is used in the preparation of vermi-compost in south India. Megascolecidae is a common family of earthworms in the Western Ghats. Earthworms in the genus *Perionyx* (family Megascolecidae) are known to inhabit compost heaps.

Fishes

In the Western Ghats, nearly one-fifth of the over 1,100 species of vertebrates—animals with backbones, are freshwater fishes representing 225 species. The only class of vertebrate animals with a greater number of species are birds. Two groups of fishes tend to contribute the most to this species richness; carps and allies (order Cypriniformes), and catfishes (order Siluriformes). Both groups of fish show enormous diversity in size and shape that may even surpass beetles. Amongst carps/barbs (family Cyprinidae), for instance, the smallest species may grow scarcely beyond a length of two centimetres (*Puntius mudumalaiensis*, weighing a few milligrams at most), while giants like *Hypselobarbus dobsoni* (barb) and *Tor khudree* (masheer) may exceed lengths of one metre and weigh over forty kilograms.

Although such diversity in size is not known in any family of catfishes in the Western Ghats, the largest species, *Wallago attu*, is known to reach lengths of two metres and weigh as much as fifty kilograms. Interestingly, one of the smallest species of catfish in India is the blind catfish (*Horaglanis krishnai*; family Clariidae) that inhabits wells in Kerala. The blind catfish does not grow beyond four centimetres.

Blind catfish are typically underground cavern species of fish in the Western Ghats that enter open wells through the subterranean springs and canals. The recent discovery of a second species, *Horaglanis alikunhii*, from Trichur district in Kerala has suggested that there could be a greater diversity in this genus of elusive catfish than known earlier. There is also a species of swamp eel (*Monopterus eapeni*) that inhabits underground caverns of Kerala. Swamp eels (family Synbranchidae) are not common in India. Of the five species known in India, three are endemic to the Western Ghats, where they are known locally. *Monopterus eapeni* and *Monopterus fossorius* are found in Kerala and *Monopterus indicus* occurs around Mumbai. All the three species are found only in the lower elevations.

The native giant danios are popular in aquarium trade

Another interesting fish is the Malabar puffer fish (*Tetraodon travancoricus*). Puffer fishes (family Tetraodontidae) are generally found in the sea. Only a few species wander into estuaries and rivers. The Malabar puffer fish that is endemic to the rivers of Kerala and southern Karnataka is a unique freshwater species. Thanks to its small size (2.5 centimetres), striking colour pattern, and habits, it is one of the most sought after species for aquarists. Similarly, the recently discovered freshwater blenny *Salarius reticulatus* (family Blenniidae) from the river Chalakudy in Kerala is as unique as the puffer fish.

Stream fishes of the Western Ghats, too, are a real delight. Some of the most colourful species such as *Puntius conchonius, Puntius melanampyx, Danio malabaricus, Danio rerio, Chela dadiburjori* and *Aplocheilus lineatus* have for long been popular in the international aquarium trade. The first four species are barbs and danios from the family Cyprinidae, while the fifth is a panchax (family Aplocheilidae); all being globally popular as aquarium fish. Others including Puntius denisonii, *Puntius setnai, Pristolepis marginatus* (family Nandidae) and *Macropodus dayi* (family Belontiidae) are also becoming popular in the international aquarium trade.

Endemic to the Western Ghats are 123 species represented by fifty-two genera. *(see table 3)* More species are likely to be added to this list in the coming years; for example, the freshwater blenny (*Salarius reticulatus*) mentioned above. Many of these are those that inhabit shallow and fast flowing streams. With the exception of one genus *Glyptothorax* (family Sisoridae) that represents catfish, all the bottom-dwelling swift water fishes belong to the order Cypriniformes, representing carps and allies. *Nemacheilus, Schistura, Bhavania, Homaloptera* and *Travancoria* are loaches that belong to the family Balitoridae. *Parapsilorhynchus* and *Garra* are 'rock-suckers' (family Cyprinidae) that have specially modified mouth parts and ventral fins, which aid them in clinging to rocks and other hard surfaces along the bottom. Since the fast flowing waters are quite rich in oxygen and are cold, torrent fishes are more sensitive to changes in temperature and aeration than others.

The black-line rasbora is found practically in all streams

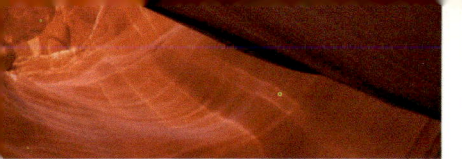

Table 3: Diversity of Endemic Fishes in the Western Ghats

Order	Family	No. of genera	No. of species
Cypriniformes (Carp, Barb, Danio, Masheer, Loach)	Cyprinidae	23	62
	Balitoridae	7	26
Siluriformes (Catfish)	Bagridae	3	6
	Siluridae	2	2
	Schilbeidae	2	2
	Sisoridae	2	7
	Clariidae	2	3
	Heteropneustidae	1	1
Beloniformes (Needle fish and allies)	Adrianichthyidae	1	1
Cyprinodontiformes (Panchax)	Aplocheilidae	1	1
Synbranchiformes (Spiny eel)	Synbranchidae	1	4
	Mastacembelidae	1	1
Perciformes (Perch, Leaf-fish, Cichlid, Gouramy, Gobies, etc.)	Chandidae	1	2
	Nandidae	1	1
	Cichlidae	1	1
	Belontidae	1	1
	Blennidae	1	1
Tetraodontiformes (Puffer fish and allies)	Tetraodontidae	1	1
Total	18	52	123

Frogs, Toads and Caecilians

Frogs and toads sing unique songs that mark their presence wherever they are. No one can ignore a calling frog or toad. The Western Ghats are full of very vocal amphibians. During the wet season, the forests and meadows reverberate with their echoing calls. Toads (*Bufo*) produce rather plaintive drumming sounds whereas the wrinkled frogs (*Nyctibatrachus*) sound quite like birds as they sing. A range of chimes and taps characterise the songs of the many species of bush and tree frogs. Although human ears cannot always distinguish the variations, frogs and toads use their songs to identify mates and breed successfully.

Estimates suggest that the majority of India's frogs, toads, and caecilians (limbless amphibians) are likely to be found in the Western Ghats with very high levels of endemism. However, only

Table 4: Diversity of Amphibians in the Western Ghats

Order	Family	Genera	Species
Anura (Frogs/Toads)	Bufonidae	Ansonia	2
		Bufo	10
		Pedostibes	1
	Microhylidae	Kaloula	1
		Melanobatrachus*	1
		Microhyla	3
		Ramanella	6
		Uperodon	2
	Nasikabatrachidae*	Nasikabatrachus*	1
	Ranidae	Micrixalus*	7
		Minervarya*	1
		Nyctibatrachus*	12
		Indirana*	8
		Fejervarya (Limnonectes)	9
		Hoplobatrachus	2
		Euphlyctis	2
		Rana	6
		Sphaerotheca (Tomopterna)	4
	Rhacophoridae	Philautus	31
		Polypedates	3
		Rhacophorus	5
Gymnophiona (Caecilians)	Ichthyophidae	Ichthyophis	7
		Uraeotyphlus*	5
	Caecilidae	Gegeneophis	7
		Indotyphlus*	2
2	7	26	138

*Note: * family/genera that are endemic*

A mating pair of Malabar gliding frogs

Photo: K A Subramanian

138 species are known today. *(see table 4)* Some of these species are those that have descended from an ancient lineage of amphibians.

Two facts together suggest that the amphibians of this hilly region are the most ancient representatives of vertebrates that India can boast of. Firstly, the recently discovered pig-nosed frog (*Nasikabatrachus sahyadrensis*) has an ancestry that may be traced back to three hundred million years ago. And, secondly, all the twenty-one species of caecilians known from the Western Ghats are endemic.

Eighty percent of the amphibian species that are found in the Western Ghats are endemic. *(see table 1)* A number of genera of amphibians are unique too. *(see table 4)* These include *Uraeotyphlus, Indotyphlus, Melanobatrachus, Micrixalus, Nyctibatrachus* and *Indirana* besides the recently added *Minervarya* and *Nasikabatrachus*. But for the first two that are caecilians, all endemic genera of amphibians are of frogs. Interestingly, the genus *Nasikabatrachus* is representative of a new family Nasikabatrachidae. This family is the most recent and a significant addition to the existing list of amphibian families of the world.

The elusive and comical *Nasikabatrachus*

Amphibians in the Western Ghats display a great diversity of sizes, shapes, colour and larval characteristics. Caecilians resemble large earthworms in many respects. The largest Indian species is *Ichthyophis malabarensis* that is endemic. Adults of this species grow to over fifty centimetres in length. The family Ranidae (true frogs) is the most diverse when it comes to size,

WESTERN GHATS | 47

shape and habits. Over thirty-six percent of all the species of frogs in Western Ghats belong to this family. As adults, the smallest representative of this family may be around 1.5 centimetres in length (as measured between the tip of the snout and the vent). *Nyctibatrachus beddomii* (earlier treated as *Nannobatrachus beddomii*) and *Minervarya sahyadris* qualify as the smallest frogs in the family as well as in Western Ghats. The largest frog is of course the Indian bullfrog (*Hoplobatrachus tigerinus*), adults of which exceed fifteen centimetres in length. The Indian bullfrog is also the largest native species in all of Asia.

Much less is known about the diversity of amphibian larvae in the Western Ghats. The most dramatic metamorphosis is exhibited by the frogs and toads (anurans). Variations in form and behaviour displayed by anuran larvae (commonly called tadpoles) are remarkable. Interestingly, the size of the tadpoles does not automatically correspond to that of the adult frogs. For instance, the common toad (*Bufo melanostictus*) that measures over fifteen centimetres in length as an adult grows from some of the smallest tadpoles. On the contrary, the bi-coloured frogs (*Rana curtipes*) that are not known to exceed 7.5 centimetres as adults are known for their large tadpoles that grow to be nearly ten centimetres in length.

Kangaroo lizard (*Otocryptis beddomei*), one of the rarest lizards

Photo: K A Subramanian

Some species of bush frogs (*Philautus*; family Rhacophoridae) do not have free-living tadpoles. Baby frogs develop directly from the eggs. One common species of bush frog that is known for this peculiar breeding habit is *Philautus variabilis*. This peculiar life history, known as 'direct development', was earlier known only in certain frogs in the tropical American rainforests. The possibility of the existence of direct-developing frogs in the Western Ghats was first suggested by Robert F. Inger after he visited the Ponmudi Hills in Kerala in 1983 with a team of amphibian biologists. More species of bush frogs that develop directly from the eggs are being discovered in Western Ghats; e.g. *Philautus glandulosus* and P*hilautus nerostagona.*

The pig-nosed *Nasikabatrachus* is apparently the most primitive frog in the region

During the last ten years, a good number of amphibian species from the Western Ghats have been identified and described for the first time. *Nasikabatrachus sahyadrensis*; Minervarya sahyadris; a species of tree frog *Polypedates pseudocruciger; Microhyla sholigari; Rhacophorus pseudomalabaricus; Nyctibatrachus hussaini; Philautus griet; Philautus luteolus; Philautus tuberohumerus; Nyctibatrachus petraeus; Philautus nerostagona; Philautus ponmudi; Philautus graminirupes*; and *Philautus bobingeri* are some of the recent additions to the list. Six species of caecilians—*Uraeotyphlus interruptus; Gegeneophis krishni; Gegeneophis danieli; Indotyphlus maharashtraensis; Gegeneophis madhavai;* and *Gegeneophis nadkarnii*—have also been added to the list during the past decade.

Turtles, Lizards and Snakes

Reptiles are some of the most elusive animals in the Western Ghats. An occasional monitor lizard (Varanus bengalensis) that crosses the road; the brilliant, red-headed rock agama (Psammophilus blanfordanus); garden lizards; skinks; and

A baby Starred Tortoise

probably a large rat snake (Ptyas mucosus) are all that is seen of reptiles. It is, therefore, hard for anyone familiar with the Western Ghats not to wonder at the fact that there are more than 160 known species, fifty-four percent of which are snakes. *(see table 5)*

Endemism in reptiles is much higher in the Western Ghats (sixty-one percent) than in India as a whole (36.7 percent), suggesting that there has been a good deal of local diversification. Snakes contribute the most to the endemic diversity. *(see table 5)* Endemic diversity at the generic and family levels is exemplified in the shield-tail snakes (family Uropeltidae). A few species of shield-tail snakes are found in Sri Lanka. Besides these, the thirty-three species of Indian shield-tail snakes are endemic. *(see table 6)*

In the Western Ghats, forty percent of all reptile species are lizards. Sixty-seven species of lizards representing fourteen genera are known till date. Over half of the species are endemic. *(see tables 5, 6)* *Salea* (family Agamidae) and *Ristella* (family

Table 5: Diversity of Reptiles in the Western Ghats

Group	No. of species	Endemic species
Turtles/tortoises	6	2
Crocodiles	1	0
Lizards	67	36
Snakes	87	61
Total	**161**	**99**

Scincidae) are examples of genera of lizards that are endemic. At the level of species, skinks (family Scincidae) and geckoes (family Gekkonidae) contribute the most to the diversity. The genus of lizards with the largest number of species in the Western Ghats is *Cnemaspis* (dwarf geckoes). Of the nineteen species known in India, sixteen occur in the Western Ghats, of which ten are endemic. It is quite likely that there are more species of dwarf geckoes that are yet to be identified in the region.

As with fishes and amphibians, there is a great diversity of size, shape and colour in reptiles as well. The smallest lizard is probably *Cnemaspis littoralis*, measuring about 6.5 centimetres including the tail. The largest lizard is, of course, the monitor lizard, *Varanus bengalensis* (family Varanidae), which attains a length of 1.75 metres. The endemic Travancore Tortoise (*Indotestudo forstenii*) is the largest tortoise, with a carapace (shell) length of thirty centimetres, and the Cochin forest cane turtle, *Geoemyda silvatica* (now known as *Vijayachelys silvatica*), which does not grow beyond thirteen centimetres, is the smallest. The largest turtle is the aquatic Leith's softshell *Aspideretes leithii* (family Trionychidae). This species that inhabits the larger rivers and reservoirs may grow to be half a metre in carapace length.

Snakes display the greatest diversity of size and shape. Both

The colourful large-scaled garden lizard

Table 6: Diversity of Endemic Reptiles in the Western Ghats

Families	Genera	No. of species
Turtles/Tortoises		
Bataguridae	*Geoemyda*	1
Testudinidae	*Indotestudo*	1
Lizard		
Gekkonidae	*Geckoella*	1
	Cnemaspis	10
	Hemidactylus	2
	Hemiphyllodactylus	1
Agamidae	*Draco*	1
	Otocryptis	1
	Salea	2
	Calotes	4
Scincidae	*Mabuya*	2
	Dasia	1
	Scincella	3
	Lygosoma	3
	Ristella	4
Lacertidae	*Ophisops*	1
Snakes		
Typhlopidae	*Typhlops*	3
Uropeltidae	*Melanophidium*	3
	Platyplecturus	2
	Teretrurus	1
	Plectrurus	3
	Brachyophidium	1
	Uropeltis	20
	Rhinophis	3
Boidae	*Eryx*	1
Colubridae	*Lycodon*	1
	Oligodon	5
	Rhabdops	1
	Xylophis	2
	Amphiesma	2
	Dendrelaphis	2
	Ahaetulla	3
	Boiga	1
Elapidae	*Callophis*	3
Viperidae	*Hypnale*	1
	Trimeresurus	3
12	**36**	**99**

the smallest snake in the world, *Ramphotyphlops braminus* (common worm snake; family Typhlopidae), and the largest venomous snake, the king cobra (*Ophiophagus hannah*; family Elapidae), are found in the Western Ghats. While the former does not exceed seventeen centimetres in length, the latter grows well over five metres. The Elapidae family also has a great range of different-sized snakes. The smallest member of the family is the slender coral snake (*Callophis melanurus*) that reaches a length of thirty-five centimetres. The king cobra belongs to the same family, and this magnitude of difference in size is something that only the family colubridae can probably match.

Unlike amphibians, fewer new species of reptiles have been added to the existing list in Western Ghats in the last decade. The worm gecko *Hemiphyllodactylus aurantiacus* that was elevated recently from the status of subspecies to species is one such addition. And the rediscovery of the Andaman garden lizard *Calotes andamanensis* from the southern Western Ghats in 1997 is yet another addition. With the recent description of a new species of dwarf gecko (*Cnemaspis anaikattiensis*), it is felt that there are greater chances of adding newer species of reptiles amongst this group of lizards.

Birds

If there is one component of the biodiversity of the Western Ghats that has been quite thoroughly studied, it is the birds. Beginning in the 1860s, British naturalists and planters started collecting and studying the birds of this region. Later surveys undertaken by Salim Ali and the many sporadic lists prepared by amateur naturalists and birdwatchers have together contributed to the existing knowledge of the diversity of birds. According to the latest reports, there are 508 species of birds in the Western Ghats. Sixty-four percent of the birds (324 species) are resident and breed locally. The rest are migratory birds, visiting the region only during the winter months. Being a narrow stretch of hills, the lower elevations on the western side are influenced by the coastal ecosystem while those on the eastern side by the freshwater ecosystems of the adjoining tableland. As a result, 144 species (twenty-eight percent) of the birds found in and around the Western Ghats are aquatic species.

The species of birds in the Western Ghats region represent nineteen orders and seventy families, as per the traditionally adopted classification. The single largest family is muscicapidae, a family of insect-eating birds, including seventy-six species of flycatchers, babblers, laughing thrushes, warblers, robins and thrushes. Around half of the species are winter visitors rendering this family the largest contributor to the diversity of migratory land birds in the region.

The Malabar whistling thrush or the 'whistling schoolboy'

The 508 bird species also vary considerably in size. The plain flowerpecker (Nilgiri flowerpecker) is the smallest forest bird measuring a mere eight centimetres, while the giants include the black eagle that exceeds eighty centimetres in length and the 130-centimetre-long great pied hornbill.

Besides variation in size, birds display the most enviable range of colours, shapes and songs. The most spectacular colours are sported by species such as the peafowl, grey junglefowl, emerald dove, Malabar trogon, black-backed kingfisher (forest three-toed kingfisher), fairy bluebird, Indian pitta, orange minivet and yellow-backed sunbird. Interestingly, these birds are representatives of different taxonomic groups and hence greatly differ in shape and habits. Some of the forest birds possess extraordinarily long and attractive tails too. The racket-tailed drongo, paradise flycatcher, peafowl and grey junglefowl are well known for their ornamental tails.

Not all birds are brightly-coloured or bear feathers that are uniquely shaped. The owls and nightjars (night birds) generally sport colour patterns that render them inconspicuous at most times. Probably the most unique of the night birds in Western Ghats is the Ceylon frogmouth. One has to see this bird to appreciate its looks and how it helps the bird in survival by providing an excellent camouflage!

Dawn breaks in the hills with songs of the Malabar whistling thrush. This bird, popularly known as the 'whistling school boy', is easily the best songster of the region. Other rivals include the white-rumped shama, magpie robin, orange-headed thrush, and the Eurasian blackbird. Drongos are the most loud and entertaining vocalists. It's a treat to hear a flock of bronzed drongos, or a racket-tailed drongo, suddenly break the silence with their repertoire of calls. Drongos are some of the finest mimics rivalled only by the shier leafbirds. Hill mynas that are so highly prized internationally as 'talking' birds are, however, not as impressive in the wilderness as the drongos or thrushes.

Endemism is lowest in birds despite their being the most diverse

The black bulbul is more of a canopy bird than its cousins in the Western Ghats

Photo: K A Subramanian

class of vertebrates in the Western Ghats. Less than three percent of all species are endemic. *(see table 1)* Even among the resident birds, only four percent are endemic. This is considerably lower than all other groups of vertebrates, including mammals.

Of the thirteen species that are endemic and the six that are largely confined to the Western Ghats *(see table 7)*, over half belong to the family muscicapidae. Nearly half of the endemic birds inhabit forests and grasslands of the higher elevations in the southern segments, suggesting that they were isolated in the hills when the temperature grew warmer. Nilgiri wood pigeon, Nilgiri pipit, Nilgiri flycatcher, Black-and-rufous flycatcher, laughing thrushes, the shortwing, and the grass bird are some of the cold-adapted endemic species. And, with the exception of the wood pigeon, all these birds have a rather restricted geographical range in the southern Western Ghats.

A peacock against a 'wall' of *Lantana* in Mudumalai WLS

Birds colonised the Western Ghats long after peninsular India became part of Asia some fifty million years ago. The present distribution patterns make it evident that most of the species of forest birds invaded from the Indo-Malayan region. A handful of species that were restricted by specialised habitats, such as the cold-adapted species mentioned above, have since evolved to become endemic species. Most others, including the low-elevation endemics, are more recent isolates. The fact that some of the endemic species such as the Malabar parakeet and rufous babbler have local populations in the eastern peninsular hills like Kolli Hills near Salem, and that birds like the fairy bluebird, rufous-bellied eagle, dollar bird and great eared nightjar, widely separated from the north-eastern populations,

Table 7: Endemic Birds of the Western Ghats

Nilgiri wood pigeon	*Columba elphinstoni**
Malabar parakeet	*Psittacula columboides**
Malabar hornbill	*Ocyceros griseus*
White-cheeked barbet	*Megalaima viridis**
White-bellied treepie	*Dendrocitta leucogastra*
Malabar lark	*Galerida malabarica*
Grey-headed bulbul	*Pycnonotus priocephalus*
Rufous babbler	*Turdoides subrufus**
Rufous-breasted laughing thrush	*Garrulax cachinnans*
Grey-breasted laughing thrush	*Garrulax jerdoni*
Wayanad laughing thrush	*Garrulax delesserti*
Black-and-rufous flycatcher	*Ficedula nigrorufa*
White-bellied blue flycatcher	*Cyornis pallipes*
Nilgiri flycatcher	*Eumyias albicaudata*
Broad-tailed grass bird	*Schoenicola platyura**
White-bellied shortwing	*Brachypteryx major*
Malabar whistling thrush	*Myiophonus horsfieldii**
Nilgiri pipit	*Anthus nilghiriensis*
Crimson-backed sunbird	*Nectarinia minima*

Note: Small and isolated populations of the species marked with an asterisk exist here and there outside the geographical limits of the Western Ghats in peninsular India. Updates on the taxonomy and nomenclature of Indian birds published after 2000 have not been adopted in this table.

have not differentiated adequately to be treated as endemic species in the Western Ghats, suggests that the isolation is rather recent, probably following the spread of agriculture.

In general, the bird fauna is comparatively poorer with respect to species diversity in the Western Ghats than in the Himalayan region. An analysis of the distribution patterns of Indian birds further reinforces this general conclusion. Of the nearly 1,300 species that have been treated as birds of the Indian sub-continent (including Nepal, Pakistan, Bhutan, Bangladesh, Srilanka and Maldives), more than seventy percent, numbering nine hundred, are known in the northeast Himalayan region. More than five hundred species of birds in the Western Ghats and the adjoining coast thus amount to a mere forty percent of bird species known in the Indian sub-continent. However, one-fourth of the nearly sixty species of birds not found outside the political limits of India have made the Western Ghats their home.

Mammals

Mammals, especially the larger species, are synonymous with wildlife in popular notion. And the Western Ghats is home to a good diversity of wildlife. The 120 species of mammals that are known in the region vary from tiny bats and mice to the mammoth-sized Asian elephant. However, the smaller mammals including bats, rodents and insectivores like the shrews contribute a far greater proportion to the diversity than the larger species. Sixty-six percent of the mammalian species belong to these three groups, and bats, represented by forty-one species, are the most diverse group of mammals found in the Western Ghats.

The Indian pipistrelle (*Pipistrellus coromandra*) is the smallest mammal. It measures less than ten centimetres in length, including the tail. The field mouse *Mus booduga* also grows to a comparable length. These tiny ones may weigh just ten to twenty grams. When compared with the elephant that may exceed 4,000 kilograms, the

Elephants in a swamp in Mudumalai WLS

difference in weight between the smallest and the largest mammal in the Western Ghats may be two to four million fold!

Including the tiger, there are over twenty species of primarily flesh-eating mammals in the Western Ghats. The flesh-eaters or carnivores include hyena, sloth bear, ratel, small and big cats (six species), dogs (three species), mongooses (four species), otters (three species), civets (four species), and marten. Of these, the Indian jackal and the grey mongoose are the most common and widespread species of carnivores.

Just like the birds, the twelve species of endemic mammals in the Western Ghats have had a very diverse ancestry. (*see table 8*) These species represent different genera, subfamily and family. The endemic bat is the sole representative of the genus *Latidens* in the whole world. Others like the Nilgiri marten and Nilgiri tahr have their closest relatives far north in the Himalayan region.

One of the three species of grey langur in the region

The pattern of endemic speciation of mammals suggests that their evolution was rather recent. The oldest of the lot is probably the bat. The langur, tahr and marten are younger and more likely the product of alternating cold and warm climate that the Indian peninsula experienced during the past 1.5 million years. Most of the other species of endemic mammals are possibly the outcome of a more recent isolation in the Western Ghats.

The above discussion is entirely based on speculation. Modern tools of molecular biology are yet to provide the correct answers to the questions on the origin of endemic mammals in the Western Ghats. The general lack of consensus on the validity of the modern molecular tools that have been adopted has kept the number of endemic species of mammals in the Western Ghats closer to what it was more than a decade ago. Although not an endemic species, because it is also found in Sri Lanka, the discovery of the Kelaart's long-clawed shrew (*Feroculus feroculus*) from the Eravikulam National Park (Kerala) and Upper Bhavani ranges (Tamil Nadu) only points to the fact that there could be yet-to-be-discovered tiny mammals lurking in the Western Ghats.

For a long while now, local forest dwellers in the southern Western Ghats have narrated encounters with a dwarf elephant called 'kal aanai' (rock elephant). A few naturalists have also

Table 8: Endemic Mammals of the Western Ghats	
Day's shrew	*Suncus dayi*
Salim Ali's fruit bat	*Latidens salimalii*
Lion-tailed macaque	*Macaca silenus*
Nilgiri langur	*Trachypithecus johnii*
Nilgiri marten	*Martes gwatkinsi*
Malabar civet	*Viverra civettina*
Brown palm civet	*Paradoxurus jerdoni*
Nilgiri tahr	*Hemitragus hylocrius*
Jungle striped squirrel	*Funambulus tristriatus*
Bonhote's mouse	*Mus famulus*
Ranjini's rat	*Rattus ranjiniae*
Malabar spiny dormouse	*Platacanthomys lasiurus*

Note: Recent changes made in the taxonomy of langur have not been adopted.

claimed that such an animal exists and have gone on to describe its unique behaviour as follows:

Herds of small elephants move around in a manner similar to the wild boar. They huddle together when alarmed, and rush into cover. In doing so, if they are on a steep slope, they practically come down on their knees and slide down.

Wildlife biologists who have spent a lifetime working on elephants have nevertheless discounted these claims, including the photographs published from time to time, as 'fakes'. The dwarf elephants are not the only mysterious animals in the Western Ghats. Higher up in the *shola* forests, many foresters, planters, forest dwellers, and a few naturalists have seen a large carnivore that resembles a cat. This big cat that apparently lacks any spots or stripes on its coat is locally called *'pukaiyan'* (smoky). Are there some large mammals that are still evading science in the Western Ghats?

A solitary Gaur Bull in Siruvani

Living Communities

When different species of organisms co-exist, they form living or biological communities. Every species is a part of one or more biological communities. The numerous ways in which species interact with each other and with the local environment, makes biological communities variable. Variations between biological communities are most often measured by their structural differences—differences in the number of species (species richness), and the abundance of each species. And when the two factors—species richness and abundance are simultaneously taken into consideration, the measure is called 'species diversity' (or diversity of species).

Although, by definition, biological communities are assemblages of various species of micro-organisms, plants and animals, ecologists have conventionally defined communities within specific taxonomic groups. Biological communities thus defined are called 'taxic'. Widely known examples of taxic communities are flowering plants, butterflies, reptiles, birds, mammals, etc., wherein the focus is on the selected groups of organisms. While the narrowed-down taxic definition of biological communities has rendered field research, especially in tropical ecosystems, more feasible, it has limited the opportunities for understanding the multitude of ecological processes that influence a community locally.

The most common fall-out of a narrowed focus on biological communities is apparent in interpretations of correlations. It is often hard to conclude whether the observed relationship between two biological communities that inhabit a specific habitat or

Lion-tailed macaque—the flag ship of the rainforest

Grooming bonnet macaques

landscape is indeed a 'cause-effect' one, or only that both are responding to some ecological factor in the same or opposite way. For instance, let us consider communities of flowering plants and birds. It has been observed that in those forests of Western Ghats where there is a greater species diversity of woody plants, there is a lower diversity of bird species. In such situations, it is hard to say whether the greater species diversity of woody plants has been responsible for the lower species diversity of birds, or that the ecological responses of woody plants and birds to the local environmental conditions have been rather different.

Despite the shortcomings, dealing with taxic communities has been popular worldwide, and all community ecological studies in the Western Ghats have adopted it because the apparent correlations have predictive value and find application in conservation planning. In the Western Ghats, it has been found that where there are more species of trees, there are also more species of ants, and where there are more species of amphibians, ants and flowering plants, there are less number of bird species. Such patterns help in identifying a range of habitats or localities, which are representative of the heterogeneity in the biodiversity of an entire landscape, and conserving which can maximise the number of species. All the research findings that are discussed in the following paragraphs have adopted the narrowed-down taxic approach to community ecology. Till such a time that long-term research covering every species and community in a landscape is affordable, taxic community ecology will prevail.

Flowering Plant Communities

Vegetation in the Western Ghats was traditionally classified into broad categories such as evergreen, semi-evergreen, coastal evergreen, Nilgiri Hills subtropical evergreen, subtropical savannah, and southern tropical deciduous, based on a combination of physiognomy (whether trees or shrubs, tall or short, etc.), local climate, and topography. Traditional classification also laid emphasis on 'climax' stages of vegetation types that varied little in structure within well-defined geo-climatic regimes.

Modern classification has, however, relied more on the community structure of plants. As a result, many sub-types have been identified within the broad categories of vegetation in a region. Thus, we have within the evergreen forests of the Western Ghats *Gordonia-Schefflera-Meliosma* series in the higher elevations; *Memecylon-Actinodaphne-Syzigium* series, *Persea-Holigarna-Diospyros* series, and *Dipterocarpus-Mesua-Palaquium* series in the medium-lower elevations; and, in the drier parts with deciduous forests, Tectona-Terminalia series, *Anogeissus latifolia-Treminalia* series, and others. The two to four generic names of trees used in the classification of the forest subtypes (or communities) suggest that species belonging to these genera dominate the plant community locally. Thus, at least nineteen flowering plant communities may be identified in the evergreen forests of the Western Ghats. (*see table 9*) Further, the recent classification of vegetation types into series or seral stages suggests that each vegetation type is a dynamic community

Showy inflorescence of *Aerides*; an orchid of the shola forests

Table 9: Flowering Plant Communities Identified in the Evergreen Forests of the Western Ghats

Wetness/Altitude	Dominant tree species
Wet evergreen/ Low elevation (0-600m ASL)	*Dipterocarpus indicus-Kingiodendron pinnatum-Strombosia ceylanicum*
	Dipterocarpus indicus-Dipterocarpus bourdilloni-Strombosia ceylanicum
	Dipterocarpus indicus-Kingiodendron pinnatum-Humboldtia brunonis
	Dipterocarpus indicus-Humboldtia brunonis-Poeciloneuron indicum
	Dipterocarpus indicus-Persea macrantha
	Dipterocarpus indicus-Diospyros candolleana-Diospyros oocarpa
	Persea macrantha-Diospyros species-oligarna species
	Diospyros species-Dysoxylum malabaricum-Persea macrantha
Wet evergreen/ Medium elevation (600-1200m ASL)	*Cullenia exarillata-Mesua ferrea-Palaquium ellipticum-Gluta travancorica*
	Cullenia exarillata-Mesua ferrea-Palaquium ellipticum
	Mesua ferrea-Palaquium ellipticum
	Poeciloneuron indicum-Palaquium ellipticum-Hopea ponga
	Memecylon umbellatum-Syzygium cumini-Actinodaphne angustifolia
Wet evergreen/ High elevation (>1200m ASL)	*Betsa indica-Gomphandra tetrandra-Litsea species*
	Schefflera species-Meliosma arnottiana-Gordonia obtuse
	Litsea species-Syzygium species Microtropis species
Evergreen forests of the drier eastern slopes	*Diospyros foliosa-Mitrephora heyneana-Miliusa species-Kingiodendron pinnatum*
	Diospyros foliosa-Mitrephora heyneana-Miliusa species
	Diospyros ovalifolia-Memecylon lushingtonii-Olea glandulifera

and is subject to changes in structure over space and time.

Communities of flowering plants change rather rapidly in the Western Ghats, from north to south and east to west, in response to the soil types, altitude, aspect, rainfall, the length of the dry season, and variations in the temperature. The species diversity of flowering plants is largely contributed by herbs, shrubs, and grasses. These plants have also been taken into consideration in defining plant communities. When shrubs are considered, the nineteen communities identified in table 9 will further split into several local sub-types. For instance, the *Persea-Holigarna-Diospyros* series may diverge into *PHD-Strobilanthes, PHD-Psychotria, PHD-Ochlandra,* and others.

The influence of rainfall on flowering plant communities is fairly well understood. Evergreen forests (or rainforests) are normally found in landscapes that receive the highest rainfall. Diversity of woody plants is generally the highest in these forests. The evergreen forests found above 1,500 metres ASL, popularly known as *sholas*, are, however, an exception. These stunted forests, elsewhere known as elfin forests wherein trees reach between fifteen and twenty metres in height are not as diverse as the lower elevation evergreen forests. Specialised woody plants that are cold adapted, such as *Schefflera, Rhodomyrtus*, and others (*see table 2*) tend to dominate *sholas*. Many rare species of herbs and woody plants are restricted to the *sholas*. Many of the trees belong to the families Lauraceae and Myrtaceae.

Sholas are considered to be 'living fossil communities' by plant ecologists. They are like oceanic islands where the process of extinction continues without any scope for immigration and colonisation of species. As a result, these forest communities are poorer in species than forests at comparable elevations elsewhere.

When equal areas are compared, it has been found that floristic richness (species richness of flowering plants) is higher in the southern Western Ghats (south of 16° N latitude) than in the north. Elsewhere, in the central Western Ghats (around 16° N latitude), the species density and richness of woody plants increases from north to south and east to west. Plots of approximately a quarter hectare may on an average hold 694

Native beauties; a wild ginger and *Thunbergia mysorensis*

woody plants representing forty species in evergreen forests, and around 300 individual plants representing twenty species in the deciduous forests. However, if flowering plants are split into trees, shrubs, herbs, and grasses and the patterns of species richness analysed, this general pattern may not hold. While trees may be most diverse in the south, plant communities in the northern Western Ghats tend to be richer in herbs and grasses.

Betelnut plantations have usurped the well-watered valleys

Changes in flowering plant community structure at scales of landscapes have largely been attributed to variations in climate and soil conditions. More locally, the flowering plant community structure is influenced by levels of human disturbance, fragmentation, and the resultant size of the fragments. Although larger fragments do support a greater richness of flowering plant species, higher levels of human disturbance tend to eliminate a number of plant species even within the largest fragments. Consequently, the area alone does not guarantee the ecological integrity of any vegetation type.

Interestingly, the overall richness of woody plants is much lower in the Western Ghats when compared with the tropical rainforests of the other parts of the world. For instance, one hectare of evergreen forests in central Western Ghats may support between thirty and sixty species, if we only consider trees with not less than thirty-centimetre girth at breast height (GBH). In Magod in northern Karnataka, there can be thirty-five species of trees with not less than ten-centimetre GBH in an area covering just 0.16 hectares. Both these estimates are considerably lower than the sixty species of trees with more than sixty-centimetre GBH known to occur in one hectare of forest in the Barro Colorado Island of Panama, ninety-eight species in 1.5 hectares of forest in Sarawak, and ninety species in 0.8 hectares of forest in New Guinea.

Ant Communities

In the forests of the Uttara Kannada district in northern Karnataka, the diversity of ant species is linked to the diversity of woody plants. Elsewhere in the Western Ghats of southern Karnataka, the presence of aggressive species such as the tree-dwelling weaver ant (*Oecophylla smaragdina*) tends to determine the species richness of local ant communities. Another study has suggested that the ants in the genus *Leptogenys* dominate terrestrial ant communities. Since the three studies were carried out in different localities, it may be inferred that the structure of ant communities vary considerably with the local ecological conditions in the Western Ghats. Judging by the differences in the habits of *Oecophylla* and *Leptogenys*, it becomes apparent that the physical and biological structure of the local plant community—canopy cover, height and density of undergrowth and species composition of woody plants—does play a role in determining the species composition of local ant communities.

Butterfly Communities

Butterfly communities in the Western Ghats are dominated by species in the family Nymphalidae (brush-foots), if only the species richness is taken into consideration. However, butterflies

Glad-eye evening brown, an elusive forest-floor butterfly

Photo: Jignasu Dolia

in the family Pieridae (whites and yellows) tend to be so numerous that the Western Ghats' butterfly community is described as a 'pierid-dominated community.' The extraordinary dominance of pierid butterflies may be attributed to the abundance of plants in the genera *Capparis, Albizia, Cassia,* and *Bauhinia.* Avenues and garden introductions of plants in the genera *Cassia* and *Bauhinia* have locally contributed to the increase in population of pierid butterflies throughout southern India. Anaikatty, a locality on the outskirts of Coimbatore, in which the study was undertaken, is part of a highly human-modified landscape, and, as such, the generalisation may be true of a larger part of the Western Ghats that has similar mosaics of habitats. The pattern may, however, be different in the better preserved rainforests such as the Kalakad-Mundanthurai Tiger Reserve (KMTR). In KMTR, the richness of butterfly species is largely contributed by the family Papilionidae (swallow-tails). Of the twenty-four species of butterflies that a recent study listed from the rainforests of KMTR, fourteen are swallow-tails. Interestingly, the KMTR study does not include even one species of pierid butterflies!

Fish Communities

Fish communities in the Western Ghats are poorly known. Studies on fish communities have been so sporadic and local that clear patterns of distribution and diversity have not yet been discerned. An assessment of the richness of the fish species in the Nilgiri Biosphere Reserve has shown that thirty percent of the ninety-two species that were observed may be rare or very rare. Although it has not been clearly discussed as to how the rarity was assessed, it may be presumed that it was based on the occurrence of each species in the fifty-six locations that were surveyed between 1993 and 1995.

Local fish communities inhabiting the higher elevations are dominated by a handful of endemic species that are adapted to torrential streams rich in oxygen and poor in productivity. The deeper and slow-flowing streams are generally richer in fish species than the shallow upstream torrents throughout the river systems in the Western Ghats. Considering the above pattern, it was felt that the east flowing streams, being slower in movement, should be richer in fish species than the west flowing. But, the only study that has specifically addressed this question has suggested that the difference is not significant. In the section of the Nilgiri Biosphere Reserve that is within Kerala, there are sixty-nine species of fish in the east flowing rivers as against sixty-eight in those that flow west. The east and west flowing river systems respectively had twenty-four and twenty-three fish species exclusive to them. Elsewhere in the Uttara Kannada district, it has been observed that the upstream and downstream fish communities are rather distinct. Fish communities are more similar in species composition across rivers than they are when the upstream and downstream segments of the same river are compared.

Denison's barb— the star of southern streams

Amphibian Communities

About half of the amphibian species that are known in the Western Ghats are localised in geographical distribution. Many species are also very patchily distributed, apparently corresponding with the distribution of their moist forest habitats. More specifically, it has been shown that caecilians prefer moist soils and hence there are more species in the rainforests and plantations of the betelnut palm. Elsewhere in the south, it seems likely that amphibian density increased with soil moisture and a greater proximity to streams.

The bi-coloured frog in an unusual attire

Community ecological studies of amphibians in the Western Ghats are rather few. Researchers in Kerala have made an attempt to analyse the community structure of amphibians within the state. One pattern that is general to Kerala, and probably elsewhere in Western Ghats, is that amphibian communities are dominated by commoner species and community structure of amphibians varies from one locality to another with respect to the number of rare and endemic species. One of the most abundant species of amphibians in Western Ghats is *Rana temporalis*. This species of frog tends to dominate most of the stream and near-stream amphibian communities with its sheer number. In the tea estates of Valparai, the bushfrog *Philautus variabilis* is the most abundant amphibian. Shifts in the pattern of dominance can be seen with changes in the habitat induced by human beings. For instance, wherever rainforests have been cleared or drastically modified, as in Agumbe and the adjoining landscapes, common aquatic species of frogs, including the skipper (*Euphlyctis cyanophlyctis*) and pond frog (*Euphlyctis hexadactylus*) turn out to be the most numerous species.

At a broader geographical scale, the patterns of distribution and richness of amphibian species are affected by altitude and rainfall. The maximum number of species of amphibians is found in the altitudinal range of eight hundred–one thousand metres ASL. Less variable temperature and shorter dry seasons have probably favoured a greater number of amphibian species in the southern Western Ghats. Since field studies of amphibians have not adopted similar methods and have been locally intensive, the geographical pattern of species richness that is apparent in the Western Ghats may well be an artefact of sampling.

Reptile Communities

Community ecology of reptiles is much less understood. Two detailed studies that are available are that of Robert Inger and colleagues in the late 1980s in Ponmudi Hills and the Wildlife Institute of India (WII) in the southern Western Ghats towards the beginning of the 21st century. Both studies are restricted to the hill ranges south of the Palghat Gap. In the Nilgiri Hills north of Palghat Gap, there have been a couple of studies of reptile communities by Salim Ali Centre for Ornithology and Natural History (SACON) and Kerala Forest Research Institute (KFRI). From the four independent studies, it is apparent that the richness of reptile species (especially garden lizards and allies) is

The common bronze-back tree snake

higher in the relatively more open and deciduous forests. The KFRI study concluded that the species richness of reptiles in Nilgiri Hills tends to fall as the altitude increases. Others also observed fewer species of reptiles at higher elevations. However, the latter authors conclude that the species richness of reptiles is the highest at mid-elevations (1000-1100 metres ASL).

Fifty-four percent of the reptile species in the Western Ghats are snakes. (*see table 5*) Studies have also shown that half of all species in the Kerala Nilgiri Hills were snakes. Contrary to the KFRI report, researchers of WII found a very low species density

The endemic Malabar rock pit viper

and richness of snakes in sample areas of twenty-five square metres size; only one out of six reptiles were snakes. In fact, the latter study has in general reported low densities of forest floor reptiles (0.26 individuals per twenty-five-square-metre sample) and reptilian presence in only 14.8 percent of the 426 sample areas in KMTR. An earlier study in Ponmudi Hills found more snakes (species as well as individuals) under terrestrial conditions. Sample areas of the small size used by WII are inadequate to study forest floor reptiles in the Western Ghats as they apparently exclude a lot of animals (especially snakes) and come up with unrealistically low estimates of the abundance of species. Poor estimates of the relative abundance of co-existing species drastically affect the analysis of the structure and diversity of biological communities.

Bird Communities

Of all living communities, birds are the most thoroughly researched in the Western Ghats. During the 1980s, one of the authors (RJRD) undertook a detailed analysis of the community structure and ecology of birds in the central Western Ghats in the Uttara Kannada district. Interestingly, bird communities are rather differently organised in the rainforests of Western Ghats than in other tropical regions. Unlike elsewhere, here, a larger number of species are found in secondary and drier forests than in the closed evergreen lowland rainforests. *Sholas* and monocultures also harbour bird communities with less number of species. However, the *sholas* (as in evergreen lowland rainforests) are home to predictable assemblages of birds, and there is a greater chance of a selected set of species being found together. Such birds have a smaller geographical range and greater conservation value than the birds in monocultures and drier secondary forests, which are drawn from a pool of widespread species that use many different habitat types.

Unlike in the rest of the tropical hill ecosystems, birds in the Western Ghats have a lower conservation value, with fewer endemic species (*see table 1*), fewer taxonomically unique species, and fewer species with specialised habitat requirement. When the 586 taxa of birds (508 species and 78 subspecies) known from south-western India are assigned conservation values using the above attributes, it turns out that the majority of birds take values that fall mid-way between low and high. Such a distribution of conservation values is due to the large number of species—the commoner ones—that have been derived from drier habitats that were widespread in the country both during ecological and geological times.

Mammal Communities

Although mammals in the Western Ghats have attracted a lot of attention from wildlife biologists, few have really tried to understand how the species organise themselves into communities. One of the earliest attempts in this regard is by ecologists at the Indian Institute of Science, Bangalore. According to his study, the evergreen rainforests are primarily suited to frugivorous and arboreal mammals such as primates and squirrels, while the deciduous forests attract the larger herbivores like gaur and deer. The drought adapted ungulates, particularly the antelopes, are best at home in the scrub jungles. In another study that pertains more or less to the same landscape, it has been shown that the biomass of large herbivorous mammals is highest in the moist deciduous forests and the teak plantations.

Community ecological studies of mammals have focused on smaller mammals, especially rodents. Systematic trapping of forest and grassland rodents in the Nilgiri Hills have indicated that the common rat (*Rattus rattus*) is the dominant species within the *shola* forests and the soft-furred field rat (*Millardia meltada*) dominates the high altitude grasslands. Both species are considered as household and agricultural pests over much of India. These two rodents along with the endemic Bonhote's mouse (*Mus famulus*) apparently show a discernable pattern of habitat choice in the higher altitudes of the Nilgiri Hills. Although sixty-one percent of the small mammal density in the higher altitude habitats was contributed by the common rat, a greater density of trees and shrubs tends to favour the Bonhote's mouse.

At least two species of shrews are found in the high altitudes of Nilgiri Hills, sharing the habitat with seven species of rodents. Of the shrews, *Suncus montanus* is abundant with as many as eleven individuals per hectare in appropriate habitat. In fact, of the nine species which comprise the high altitude rodent-shrew community, *Suncus montanus* ranks second in overall abundance. While this species of shrew occasionally shares the habitat with the soft-furred field rat in the grasslands, the endemic shrew *Suncus dayi* is more of a *shola* species. With the exception of the soft-furred field rat, all the mammals that are part of the high altitude rodent-shrew community tend to avoid the open grasslands.

Ecological Patterns

Studies on the patterns of distribution and diversity of living communities in the Western Ghats have been local and sporadic. Most studies have been of short duration and have adopted different field methods. Nevertheless, there are a few consistent ecological patterns that the living communities display.

Clear cascades like this one are no longer common

Firstly, there is an apparent correspondence between the diversity of some groups of organisms. Localities that are the richest in woody plants may also support the most species-rich communities of ants, amphibians, small carnivores, and frugivorous arboreal mammals. The most species-rich communities of butterflies, reptiles, birds, and large mammals are often associated with the moist deciduous and secondary forests where the species richness, density as well as diversity of plants are lower.

Secondly, it has been observed that species richness in communities of less mobile organisms such as woody plants and amphibians is influenced much more by the altitude and the length of the dry season than in communities of highly mobile organisms like birds.

Thirdly, the ways in which local communities of certain organisms are organised tend to predict the structure of certain

Eucalyptus plantations have taken over the high altitude grasslands locally

associated communities. For instance, the structure and species composition of woody plants rather than the species richness, better predict the species composition of local bird communities. In other words, it is easier to predict whether the bird community will include diverse guilds—sets of species with similar ecological needs—by looking at the density, canopy cover, and the abundance of certain species of woody plants in forests rather than by trying to relate the number of woody plant species with the number of bird species locally. In fact, it has been shown that at low and medium elevations, forests with the greatest diversity of woody plants may support the lowest diversity of birds.

Finally, as will emerge clearly in the sections that follow, living communities in the Western Ghats have responded differently to local human impacts.

People, Culture and History

The First Human Invaders

It is believed that the antiquity of human life in south India goes back to the Palaeolithic age about twelve thousand years ago. (*see table 10*) Early anthropologists discern two streams of cultures during this phase—one, the Soan Culture centred in the North-West, and the other, the Madras Industry based in the South-East. South India has also witnessed a cultural continuity through the subsequent stages to the present as evidenced by the numerous artefacts, neolithic pastoral traditions, and megalithic burials. Stone tools used by the Palaeolithic people have been excavated in the river valleys of Palakkad (Palghat), Mallapuram and Dakshina Kannada districts. Palaeolithic artefacts have also been found in and around Mysore, Chikmagalur and Shimoga districts of western Karnataka.

Paniyar women and children within Mudumalai WLS

Kurumba women gathering tubers

WESTERN GHATS | 77

Table 10: Chronology of Human Ecological Events in the Western Ghats

Years before Present (ybp)	Ecological events
>12,000	Hunting and gathering
12,000–5,000	Hunting-gathering, use of fire, forest decline, and increase in savanna
5,000–3,000	Agro-pastoralism in the Deccan, vegetation change in the Nilgiri Hills, coastal deforestation, use of iron, Harappan and Deccan immigrants come into the Western Ghats
3,000–1,000	Agro-pastoralism, Western Ghats neoliths, shifting cultivation, decline in primary forests, sacred groves, extraction of spices and timber
1,000–200	European trade, extraction of timber for ship building, increase in spice trade, organised agriculture, shifting cultivation continues
200–100	Increased timber harvest, state forestry begins, shifting cultivation regulated, natural teak depleted, plantations initiated
<100	Timber harvest intensified, timber stocks depleted, conservation by state, mines, dams, townships

Mesolithic sites have been discovered around the river Mandovi in Goa. Charcoal beds dating back to five thousand years in Tenmalai (southern Western Ghats) suggest that humans burnt forests around this time. During the new stone age (5,000-3,000 years ago), man herded cattle, sheep, and goats in and around the Western Ghats. Rainfed crops including millets and horse gram were generally cultivated; in Maharashtra the Jorwe people also cultivated wet rice. Shifting cultivation was apparently the form of agriculture that predominated till recently. Crops such as *Eleucine coracana*, *Cajanus cajan*, *Ricinus communis* and *Panicum sumatrense* were mainly cultivated in this traditional system of agriculture.

The impact of humans in this period would have been minimal as they hunted and gathered, and occasionally used fire to clear forests, especially the dry types. It was only after iron was discovered and began to be used around 1000 BC that the axe started playing a role in cutting down the evergreen forests. Mastery over the use of fire, and iron tools probably favoured the

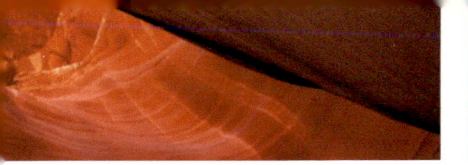

Rice cultivation in the Mudumalai WLS which are the hotspots of man-elephant conflicts

early colonisation of the cold and wet mountains. The Todas had apparently reached the upper reaches of the Nilgiri Hills as early as 200 BC. They brought with them the first domestic cattle. The extensive pastures available in the mountain grasslands and the fewer carnivores in the higher reaches made it conducive for the pastoral Todas to settle at elevations above 1,800 metres ASL in the Western Ghats.

The Todas did not use the plough. They considered the earth to be their mother and forbidded the running of a ploughshare through her bosom. They only gathered food and grazed cattle. While the impact of the Todas was very small and local in the Nilgiri Hills, there were other human cultures that had already started modifying the vegetation along the western sides. Samples of fossilised pollen collected from the marine cores off the coasts of the Uttara Kannada district have suggested that around 3,500 years ago, there was a sharp increase in grasslands at lower elevations. Like elsewhere in India, the spread of savannas is perhaps the result of human intervention in forested landscapes.

Cultural Landscapes

Cultural landscapes started evolving in peninsular India at least three thousand years ago. The cultural landscapes in which the early Tamil societies evolved can be traced back to the period of the Sangam literature (300 BC–300 AD). Sangam was a mythical literary convocation held at Madurai, the capital city of the Pandyas, in which Tamil poets of old sang about already ancient traditions. It was after this convocation that South India's first historic period from 300 BC to 300 AD was defined and christened as Sangam. The Sangam period—a time coincident with the late neolithic period marked the last stages of the early tribals—Eyinars, Kurumbars, and Vedars as also the emergence of the second-line of tribes—Malavars, Kosars and Kongars.

Sangam liteature portrays the diversity in both the ecosystem and society, with its attendant localism of social experience and identity. This not only typified the south Indian culture during that period, but also laid the foundation for the coming generations. The study of Sangam by Tamil scholars has been extensive for its poetic genre. Commentaries, notably by U.V. Swaminatha Iyer in the 1900s and Illakkuvanar in 1963, have enabled scholars of other languages to understand and analyse Sangam. While certain dimensions of Sangam are still under debate, it is generally agreed that the compilation laid emphasis on capturing the socio-ecological system of the ancient times by employing the poetic genre. This is best described in one of the early treatises, *Tolkappiyam*.

Tolkappiyam, the most ancient among the surviving Tamil treatises from that period, seems to have been composed during 1000–600 BC. This treatise is the very foundation of the classical edifice of which the Sangam works form a significant part. *Tolkappiyam* describes the various kinds of cultural landscapes that the early Tamils recognised under a collective system called

Plastic has penetrated even the remotest villages in Mudumalai

'Tinai', which is expounded in the third section titled, *Porul Atikaaram*. This continued to be the bedrock of the life of Tamils and all the systems that they developed, until the new order of caste emerged and forced the Tinai into obscurity.

Tinai is interpreted as a firm conglomeration—an ecosystem where people and nature co-evolve. The Western Ghats have been classified under the mountainous cultural landscapes called Kurinji. The word 'Kurinji' is the Tamil name for *Strobilanthes* species—the blue flowers that some say have given the Nilgiri Hills or the Blue Mountains its name.

A *Kumri maratti* drummer wearing a head gear of plastic flowers

The mountainous cultural landscapes, besides being characterised by the blue flowers of *Strobilanthes kunthianus* or Kurinji, have been described as having the following ecological elements—cold seasons, early frost, waterfalls, cave-dwelling hill tribes that collected honey and dug out tubers for food, gardens where millets were cultivated, forests that provided habitat to valuable timber, including sandalwood and wildlife such as elephants, bears, monkeys, wild pigs, junglefowl, peafowl, parakeets, and horned owls. Early human societies that typically inhabited the Kurinji landscape were known as Kuravar, Punavar, Malavar, and Iravukar.

The early hill-dwelling human societies probably diversified into many more endogamous tribes or caste-groups that filled specific occupational niches. For example, within the large landscape that has been designated as the Nilgiri Biosphere

Reserve, there are at least twenty-nine such endogamous human communities. Some of these communities still subsist by hunting wildlife such as monkeys, small mammals, and fish. These include the Aranadan, Cholanaicken, Irular, Karunaicken, Kurichian, Kurumba, Malaimalasar, Malasar, and Pani Yerava. Others like Allar, Adiyan, Edanadan Chetti, Karimpalan, Kotta, Malayan, Panjanai Yerava, Urali, and Kader have continued collecting non-timber forest produce to supplement agriculture. The above list represents the broad categorisation of the tribal communities inhabiting the Western Ghats, and is in some sense rather superficial. The finer categorisation that the tribes use to distinguish themselves, which is most noticeable amongst the Kurumbas, also reflects how the indigenous communities partitioned natural resources.

Photo: R Prabhakar

A *toda* family in Nilgiri Hills

Pepper cultivation within Mudumalai WLS

Endogamous human communities that are designated as tribes continue to survive throughout the Western Ghats. In the hills and forests of Maharashtra there are Bhil, Pawara, Konkana, Mahadeo Koli, Malhar Koli, Warli, Katkari, and Thakar. These and many other forest-dwelling communities have created and nurtured a wide range of cultural landscapes throughout the Western Ghats.

82 | WESTERN GHATS

From Monarchs to the British Raj

The Sangam treatises have a number of verses that describe the early Tamil chieftains and warriors. The fiefdoms of the early chieftains covered much of the southern Western Ghats. The world of Tamil culture (Tamilagam) has been described as extending from Tiruvengadam (probably the present Tirupati or Tirumala in Andhra Pradesh) to Kanyakumari in the south and bounded by the seas on the east and the west. Traditionally, this region was subdivided into five Nadus (kingdoms)—Chola Nadu, Pandya Nadu, Chera Nadu, Tontai Nadu, and Kongu Nadu. Tontai Nadu is relatively lesser known and Kongu Nadu is referred to as a separate geographical region ruled by an overlord loyal to one of the first three Nadus.

The boundaries of the Nadus changed over time because of the countless number of wars between the Cheras, Cholas, and Pandyas, besides the intermittent wars between the minor kings and chieftains. The expanse of each of these Nadus was indicative of the power the kingdoms exerted over Tamilagam. Table 11 summarises what is broadly agreed upon as the boundaries of the five kingdoms.

Kumri maratti dancers in a festive mood in Uttara Kannada

Table 11: Boundaries of the Major Kingdoms of Tamilagam

The Regions	Boundaries			
	North	South	East	West
Pandya	Vellaru[2]	Kumari[2]	Sea	Open Plain
Chola	Elam[2]	Vellaru[2]	Sea	Kottakarai[3]
Cheras	Palani[2]	Sencottah[2]	Kodaiyar[2]	Calicut[3]
Tontai	Vengadam[1]	Pinaki[1]	Sea	Ghats
Kongu	Talamalai[2]	Palani hills[2]	Mattilkarai[2]	Velliyangiri[3]

Note: 1-Andhra Pradesh; 2-Tamilnadu; 3-Kerala

More specifically, the Kongu region is comprised of the following present-day administrative units—the Nilgiris, Coimbatore district (except the mountainous areas of Gobichettipalayam, Bhavani, Pollachi, and Udumalpet taluks), Karur taluk, Palani taluk, Nammakkal, Tiruchangodu, and Sankari taluks of Salem district. The region, therefore, encompasses a large tract of land including portions of the southern Western Ghats and the adjoining plateaus, three passes, especially in the south-eastern direction, the Eastern Ghats and the intermittent plains. In the ancient scheme of classification of lands, Kongu Nadu by virtue of having forty-nine hills within its boundaries was a Kurinji landscape.

Tolkappiyam also divided Tamilagam on the basis of dialects into thirteen Nadus. While Sentamil Nadu (the land of chaste Tamil) was defined as that area which was on the banks of river Vaigai, including the city of Madurai, the rest of the Nadus were spread across the Tamilagam. It is plausible that the Nilgiris and the adjoining areas were referred to as Ceeta (cold) Nadu and Malai (hilly) Nadu. Incidentally, the hill-plateau region of the state of Karnataka that includes the central

A traditional settlement inside the Mudumalai WLS

Western Ghats is formally classified as 'Malnaad'.

The Kongu region, notably the Malabar Coast, Wayanad, the Nilgiris, the southern portion of Coimbatore district, and part of Tirunelveli district, was largely under the Cheras, although some authors contend that there was the presence of a Satavahana ruler on the Nilgiris during the same time. Literary evidence of the Chera rule over Nilgiris is found in *Paditrupattu* and *Silapadikaram*. Interestingly, scholars of Kongu history, notably Arockiaswami, argue that records and writings during the colonial period, including those of Buchanan, referred to Kongu Nadu and Chera Nadu interchangeably.

The early reign of the Cheras was constantly in turmoil, largely due to the Malavars—a tribe that inhabited the hilly regions of Kongu, and believed to be great warriors adept at handling elephants. These Malavar chieftains together are believed to have launched a series of battles, and annexed parts of the Chera country. In a bid to curb their growing influence, Perumcheral Irumporai, the Chera king, first induced Kari, a Velir chieftain of Tirukovilur (currently in the North Arcot district of Tamil Nadu), to invade parts of the Eastern Ghats

Kaliappan, an excellent oarsman, streering a *parisal* down the River Bhavani

during 25-50 AD and subsequently re-annexed the region.

As a result, a prolonged battle was fought between Perumcheral and Atiyaman, a Malavar chief. Both Atiyaman and his son Elini were killed in this battle, enabling Perumcheral to establish the Chera monopoly over *Kongu*. This battle is referred to in a work called the *Tagadur Yattirai*, of which only a few stanzas have survived.

Also of significance to Kongu is the second reign of the Cheras at the beginning of the ninth century AD. This reign is identified with King Kulasekara Varman. He was one of the twelve eminent Vaishnavite saints (Alwars) and was better known as Kulasekara Alwar. The dynasty was also called the Perumal dynasty. The king called himself Kongar Koman, clearly highlighting the control of the Cheras over Kongu.

The Chera monopoly over Kongu was contested not only by the Cholas, Pandyas and Gangas, but also by other chieftains. The most dominant of these chieftains were the Velir princes, of whom six great families could be distinguished. Historians like Arockiasami consider Velirs to be the progenitors of the Vellalars. More recently, the Kongu Nadu was subjected to influxes from people belonging to the Vijayanagar Empire and Mysore, especially Tipu Sultan in the eighteenth century.

Despite being overshadowed politically by its neighbours,

A shrine venerated by the moundadan shetty community within Mudumalai WLS

Paniyar children

Kongu Nadu is better defined than the other four Nadus of Tamilagam in geographical terms. The total area of the ancient Kongu was approximately 39,000 square kilometres, divided into twenty-four sub-nadus. It was bordered by hill ranges on all sides, except the south-east. And it is from this direction that many of the invasions into Kongu have taken place.

Kongu Nadu has had a rather variegated political history, primarily due to the following two reasons. One, it did not hold the status of an independent empire in the ancient scheme of classification. It was a separate geographical region ruled by an overlord loyal to one of the major dynasties of Tamilagam. And, two, several important trade routes passed through this region towards the west coast of India. The traders carried a variety of goods including iron and iron implements, which eventually found their way to Rome or Egypt. A number of battles were fought for gaining supremacy over the region and some of the major dynasties established their reign over this land. Intermittently, there were also a number of uprisings of feudal lords, chieftains, and minor kings. Table 12 describes the major dynasties that ruled over Kongu, highlighting those attributes that have been significant to the ecological history of the southern Western Ghats, specifically the Nilgiris and adjoining hills.

Ready-made garments have come in handy for this *Paniyar* woman and child

Table 12: Chronology of Dynasties that Ruled Kongu-Nilgiris

Dynasties	Approximate time frame	Attributes/Scenario
Vedars, Eyinars, and Malavars	Until 75 AD	• Presence of dense forests and large mammals like the elephants • Migration into the hills • Colonisation of agriculture, especially millets, rice, sugarcane, bananas, and spices • Social organisation as indicated by clans and community hunting • Presence of precious metals
Cheras	Until 200 AD	• Coincident with the end of the Sangam period, possible influx of people from the plains • Resident armies that included elephants
Rashtrakutas	250–405 AD	• Possible influence of Jainism • Importance to cavalry
Gangas	405–750 AD	• First records of land revenue settlement; land taxes fixed on the basis of soil fertility as determined from the yields of the previous three years • Recognition of lands totally exempted from taxation and categorised as Sarvamanya, Tribhoga and Brahmadeya
Kadambas		• Insignificant reign—restricted to Wayanad
Pandyas	680–710 AD	• One conquest using a cavalry comprising elephants
Cheras of the Perumal Dynasty	790–820 AD	• No direct influence on Nilgiris • Influence of Brahminic traditions
Cholas	985–1014 AD	• Re-emergence of Malavar supremacy • Definition of land ownership, regularisation of assessment, land quality parameters, etc.
Hoysalas	1117–1352 AD	• Records on Todas—the pastoral tribe—and Kurumbas • Resistance from local inhabitants over the rule • Southward invasion of Malik Kafur, the general of Allaudin Khilji; Nilgiris not conquered
Vijayanagar	1340–1565 AD From 1530 AD, under the Nayaks (vassals appointed by the Vijayanagar rulers)	• Most turbulent period • The era of poligars—feudal system of land revenue with oppressive land tax systems • Two systems for administration—Ummatur held control over Mudumalai–Gudalur • Concrete reference to Mudmalai—inscription of 1527 reads—'Krishna Raya Nayaka… granted to a certain person the village of Masanahally in Bayalnadu… with eight rights, full possession to be enjoyed by him and his descendents as long as the sun and moon endure.' Masanahally is now called Masinagudi.

		• Trade in timber, foodgrains, fruits and spices
Mysore kings	1714–1732 AD	• Vassal king takes over Wayanad, goes on a rampage • Poligars continue with unreasonable taxes and extraction modes • Nellialam—a hamlet close to Mudumalai—was an abode of rest
Hyder Ali and Tipu Sultan	1748–1792 AD	• Area divided into three geographical tracts—Baramahal, Balaghat and Talaghat • Land tax was the major source of income, with arbitrary rates of assessment • Forests explored for sandalwood • Annexed by the British in the year 1792 during the Mysore wars

Human Activity and Ecological Change

Taming the Wilderness

A long history of human-in-nature situation resulted in the evolution of several types of cultural landscapes in the Western Ghats. The persistent ecological transformations that the cultural landscapes underwent, however, led to irreversible changes over vast areas causing ecosystems to flip from one state to another. Thus, rainforests were transformed into barren laterite beds that support plant life only for a short while after the rains; deciduous forests have turned into scrub jungles; hills that were once covered with tall forests have today been reduced to mere pastures. And vast parts of the landscape that were ecologically sustainable have flipped into a state where the ecosystem processes are entirely regulated by humans—for example, the estates.

Ecosystem flips did not take place overnight. They went through certain stages of transformation. According to ecologists, one or more of the following may in succession have led to the ecosystem flip.

- Transformation of the landscape elements, especially vegetation into one that offers more scope for hunting and gathering of food, minimises risks of injuries and death caused by accidents or wild animals, provides greater opportunity to domesticate and cultivate wild animals and plants respectively, and minimises the risk of crop/livestock losses;
- Direct conflicts and resultant adaptive strategies that lead to the reduction or even elimination of 'harmful' plants and animals in the landscape;
- A newly created 'soft landscape' wherein certain habitats and species (especially plants) are favoured after the elimination or displacement of others and which is actively managed by

Rainforests intercropped with cardamom in Kerala

an organised social system. Such a system will show a shift in the values placed on biodiversity—favouring some and disregarding others as dictated by the inherent fondness and dislike for living organisms, and the rapidly changing human needs and aspirations.

Human influences have had different scales of impacts on the biodiversity of the Western Ghats. Species extinctions in Western Ghats have been local and certainly coincident with the recent changes in land use. Unique landscape elements such as the *Myristica* swamps gave way to the cultivation of rice. Along with the swamps, trees such as *Myristica fatua, Gymnacranthera carnatica, Semecarpus auriculata* (*Semecarpus kathlekanensis*) and the palm *Pinanga dicksonii* disappeared locally. The use of fire to clear forests for cultivation has also had a major influence on the forests. The spread of bamboo and deciduous trees in the region would have been aided by this human practice. Widespread occurrence of fire-tolerant woody plants such as *Acacia catechu, Careya arborea, Dalbergia latifolia, Dillenia pentagyna, Schleichera oleosa, Tectona grandis, Treminalia* species, and *Xylia xylocarpa* suggests that the forests have experienced extensive fires in the past.

Reduction in the extent of forests has led to the local loss of

A scenic man-made lake in Ulttara Kannada

plants and animals. Fragmentation and a greater intensity of human disturbance have drastically reduced the diversity of flowering plants locally and favoured the invasion of non-native shrubs in the understorey, thereby increasing the overall stem density.

In selectively logged evergreen forests, the woody plant species diversity has declined. This has been accompanied by the loss of certain plant species of greater economic value such as *Syzigium gardneri, Myristica malabarica, Calophyllum polyanthum, Dysoxylum malabaricum,* and *Polyalthia fragrans.* Forest birds that have locally been exterminated due to disturbance and fragmentation are *Zoothera dauma* (ground thrush), *Psittacula eupatria* (parakeet), *Picus myrmecophoneus* (woodpecker), *Treron bicincta* (pigeon), and *Aethopyga siparaja* (sunbird).

Other organisms have responded to human disturbance rather differently. Moderate levels of disturbance have increased the richness of flowering plant species in the Anaimalai Hills. Selective logging, and the consequent lower tree and canopy density have locally increased the number of species of butterflies, lizards, and birds. Although the exact characteristics of the lizard species that have contributed to the higher diversity in logged forests have not been discussed, it has been shown that the diversity of butterflies and birds increase locally due to the invasion of 'ubiquitous' species.

Nutmeg—a spice that has many wild relatives in the region

Between 1920 and 1960, the rate at which the forests were lost in the Western Ghats was 0.07 percent annually. However, the rate had leaped to 0.33 percent annually by 1990. The loss of forest cover has been more drastic locally. In Kerala, forty-seven percent of the evergreen and semi-evergreen forests were lost in just thirty years.

The loss of closed canopy rainforests has been detrimental to flowering plants. Many invasive species of plants have found their way into natural forests. Important amongst these are *Lantana camara* (var *aculeata*), *Eupatorium odoratum, Mikania cordata,* and *Parthenium hysterophorus*. Wattle (*Acacia species*) once introduced for the extraction of tannin in the higher hills is today a major threat to the *sholas* and grasslands at these altitudes.

The impact of these exotic plants on the ecosystem and biodiversity generated a lot of debate. *Lantana*, which soon naturalised itself by taking advantage of the small frugivorous birds that dispersed its seeds far and wide, proved to be a practical nuisance by creating barriers to the movement of mammals and in summer, a major cause for the spread of forest fires. However, concerns that *Lantana* prevents forest regeneration have not been substantiated. One study carried out in the BRT Hills has shown that contrary to general predictions, the presence of *Lantana camara* has not been detrimental to local woody plant species richness.

High altitude bogs like this one are storehouses of fossilised pollen

Loss of rainforest canopy and fragmentation of once extensive habitats have had the most adverse impact on the endemic species of primates. The lion-tailed macaque is sensitive to the shape and orientation of the forest fragments. Primate experts have argued that small canopy openings of size 0.5 square kilometres are adequate to prevent the movement of foraging troops. However, their conclusion is certainly premature as a fairly large troop of the macaque was recently observed beyond the periphery of the Periyar Tiger Reserve foraging within human habitation, perched on cultivated silk cotton trees and in the absence of closed canopy rainforests. Local residents confirmed that the troop was regularly visiting these secondary habitats.

Opening of the canopy due to selective removal of trees has led to the loss of foodstuff for the Nilgiri langur in the southern Western Ghats. Such disturbances resulted in a decrease in birth rate and increase in death rate among the troop of langur that A. J. T. Johnsingh and his student studied. The conclusion of the study may also be premature as the Nilgiri langur has been observed in more than one landscape freely foraging with the common (grey) langur. Interestingly, in all these landscapes the mixed troops consist of langur that are intermediate in size and colour suggesting that the two species interbreed in nature! Further, in the outskirts of Ooty (Nilgiris), the Nilgiri Langur has been observed resting and feeding on the ground within built-up areas much as the commoner Bonnet Macaque does.

Elsewhere, opening the forest canopy by selective or clear felling has probably favoured the spread of the common rat in the higher altitudes. The spread of grasslands has taken the soft-furred field rat, an agricultural pest, to the mountains in the Western Ghats.

Gardens that Spread

Early gardens were characterised by the presence of banana plants, fruit trees like jackfruit and jamun, tubers including yam (*Dioscorea, Amorphophallus*), taro (*Colocasia*), green vegetables, pulses, spices such as cardamom and black pepper, and a number of

Fire-resistant bracken and invasive asters encroach montane grasslands

WESTERN GHATS | 95

millets. Rice was grown in the wet valleys. Selection to suit local ecological conditions led to the evolution of a great genetic diversity in a number of species of local plants. The early gardens, thus, proved to be nurseries of the enormous diversity of land races that are known today.

Hill agriculture in the Western Ghats is at present dominated by estates—chiefly of tea, coffee, rubber, and monocultures of various tree species, including the recently introduced oil palm. For instance, the Nilgiri district with a total area of 2,549 square kilometres had around one thousand square kilometres under various forms of cultivation even twenty years ago. Along the coast, other exotic trees found their way into beaches and the littoral forests. Teak was first raised as a monoculture in 1840. The first teak plantation in Kerala was established in Nilambur in 1844. *Casuarina* plantations first appeared in the Uttara Kannada district between 1868 and 1869. Till then the forest plantations were of native species. Over the years, plantations of eucalyptus, cinchona, wattle, rubber, clove, and cashew have displaced extensive patches of natural forests throughout the Western Ghats.

Typical tahr habitat

Around twenty years ago, not less than 1,500 square kilometres were under coffee cultivation, and 825 square kilometres under cardamom. The cultivation of cardamom has been a traditional practice dating back to over two thousand years in the Western Ghats. Coffee, however, is more recent. Legend has it that a Muslim pilgrim called Baba Budan brought seven coffee seeds of the *Arabica* variety from Yemen in the seventeenth century and planted them in his hermitage in Chikmagalur. Coffee was then introduced into Kodagu (Coorg). Large-scale planting of coffee began only in 1854 after the British established themselves in Kodagu.

Coffee is usually grown in the shade. Over most parts of the Western Ghats, the native trees have been retained for providing shade in coffee plantations. Such a practice has proved less detrimental to biodiversity than other forms of commercial agriculture in which the entire landscape is cleared before the crop is raised. The large numbers of native tree species that have thus been retained in the traditional coffee estates have matured, with the extensive canopy offering ideal habitats for a great diversity of animals.

Small patches of rainforests thrive within private estates

Photo: Jignasu Dolia

Tea, on the contrary, demands abundant sunlight and therefore is planted after the entire area is cleared of all other vegetation. Tea gardens are spread between 300 and 2,300 metres ASL. Around twenty years ago, tea plantations covered 750 square kilometres in areas above an altitude of 1,500 metres ASL. Although tea had been introduced in parts of Western Ghats as early as the 1830s, the opening of the Suez Canal in 1860 provided greater trade opportunities. A major influx of labourers came in the wake of increasing tea cultivation. This was buttressed on the other side by forced migration due to famine in the plains of Tamil Nadu in 1870, and aided by the Christian missionaries. Another wave of immigration of settlers followed into the tea growing landscapes during 1940-1950, significantly increasing the local human population.

Tea has also been raised and maintained by the Tamil Nadu Forest Department. For instance, parts of Nilgiri and the Anaimalai hills have extensive tea plantations that are owned by the Forest Department and managed by TANTEA, an agency established exclusively for this purpose. These plantations were part of the means adopted to provide labour and livelihood opportunities to the hundreds of Sri Lankan Tamils who have been formally provided refuge in the Western Ghats.

Today, the area planted with tea in the Western Ghats amounts to only eighteen percent of the country's total tea cultivation. There is, however, little scope for increase in the cultivated area as the recent losses faced by the tea industry has forced planters including multinational corporations to abandon the existing estates.

Arenga wightii—a large understorey palm that is endemic to the region

Apart from the introduction of commercially significant plants, a number of alien plant species have also invaded the landscape. The British colonists spread over most of the Western Ghats between the late 1700s and the early 1800s. The Nilgiri

Hills were colonised only in 1813, almost two thousand years after the Todas first inhabited it. In 1832, the Australian wattles (*Acacia species*) were brought in. Eucalyptus was first planted in the Nilgiris in 1843. By 1922, potato cultivation had also been extensively introduced.

Much of the exotic flora in the Nilgiri Hills, especially those of temperate origin, came in only after the British made Ooty the summer capital of the Madras Presidency in 1866. Around 400-500 species of alien plants have been reported from the Nilgiri Hills alone. A large number of ornamental plants of temperate (Alpine) origin have since run wild in the higher elevations. In the Palani Hills, there are six hundred such species, especially around Kodaikanal. Amongst the hundreds of European invasive plants, the popular 'everlasting flower' (*Helichrysum bracteatum*) has been the most sought after species as the dried flowers stay intact for years and adorn many a home not only in the Western Ghats but throughout the country.

A mature tree fern *(Cyathea)*

Muddy Waters

The Western Ghats receive an average annual rainfall of around two hundred centimetres. Due to the topography, the entire landscape is well-watered with numerous streams and rivers. Natural wetlands (bogs) in the higher elevations, and swamps in the mid and low elevation rainforests have enriched the habitat diversity in the landscape. Further, the numerous waterfalls have created unique microhabitats for plants, insects, fish, amphibians, and even birds.

The cold and clear waters that flow out of the perennial springs have sustained biodiversity and human communities over the past millennia. Unfortunately however, the crystal clear waters that once flowed throughout the Western Ghats are today hard to find. Wherever present, they have turned seasonal in nature, coming to life with the rains and flowing for a short while thereafter.

Loss of forests and canopy has rendered most first order streams seasonal. These clear flowing streams tend to stagnate in summer and as a consequence turn coloured. Excessive soil erosion and run-off that take place higher up in the slopes have made the waters at the lower elevations muddy and enriched with organic matter, encouraging the unhealthy growth of algae. Added to the small-scale changes in land use that have caused soil to erode, fertilisers to leach, and pesticides to pollute the waters, there are large-scale damages due to the effluents that run out of factories processing rubber, coffee, tea, and other horticultural products. The fenny (an indigenous alcoholic drink) industry in Goa has polluted many streams locally. Electrochemical industries in the Nilgiri Hills proved to be a major threat to the natural waters. Lakes that were created for recreation as that in Ooty and Kodaikanal have been the most readily available sinks for urban sewage. These and the many other forms of human

A small dam surrounded by degraded dry forests

abuse of aquatic habitats have muddied the crystal clear waters that once filled the vast expanse of the Western Ghats.

The worst abuse of water has been through the construction of dams. Hundreds of small and big dams have completely upset the flow of water and hydrological cycles in the Western Ghats. Not a single river has survived these contraptions of engineers. The different states through which the Western Ghats (and its rivers) run have had different policies towards the construction and use of dams and reservoirs. Most early dams were meant to generate power. The largest concentration of dams meant to generate hydroelectricity is probably in the Nilgiri Hills. However, Maharashtra tops in the list of the number of dams constructed. Estimates have placed the number of dams in Maharashtra at around 630. Not all dams are located in the Western Ghats. Yet, since they obstruct the flow of water in the rivers that originate in the hills, they lead to both hydrological and ecological changes upstream.

Riparian forests are the most common victims of hydroelectric projects

Muddy waters result from poor flow, stagnation, and organic enrichment due to run-off and erosion. Muddy waters tend to be warmer due to the suspended particulate matter. They permit poor entry of light and hence interfere with the productivity of water. Muddy waters are poor in dissolved oxygen as well. The apparent physical and chemical changes that these waters undergo affect aquatic biodiversity drastically.

Current knowledge has made it rather evident that the aquatic ecosystem makes the greatest contribution towards the endemic biodiversity of Western Ghats. (*see table 1*) Field observations and collections have supported taxonomists' opinion that there can be many yet-to-be-discovered species of aquatic animals, especially amphibians and fishes, in the Western Ghats. The process of decimation of this unique aquatic biodiversity starts with the local loss of aquatic invertebrates—snails, amphibian larvae and fish. Even in the apparently 'clean' streams, it has been observed that the aquatic invertebrates have disappeared. Although the immediate blame can be laid on pesticides, the overall lack of systematically collected data on the ecological impacts of pesticides has made it difficult to substantiate this popular notion in the Western Ghats.

Thorns and Vermin

Thorns flourish in forests interfered by humans. Prolific and stunted growth of bamboos, cane, and a number of other species of thorny plants is clearly the result of excessive human interference in the forests of the Western Ghats. Plants that bear thorns such as *Flacourtia montana, Pterolobium hexapetalum, Moullava spicata*, latex as well as poison-producing ones such as *Holigarna* species, *Strychnos* species, and *Sapium insigne* are often the most abundant plants in the humid landscapes that are under constant human pressure. In drier habitats, the common obnoxious plants are stunted bamboo, *Lantana camara, Randia* species, *Acacia* species, cacti (*Opuntia*), and cacti-like *Euphorbia* species. These plants survive only because they are not cut for fuel or grazed by cattle.

Just as human interference has favoured the spread of obnoxious plants, including the many alien invasive species, there are many species of animals too that have gained the status of vermin in the Western Ghats. The aquatic ecosystems are already affected by the invasion of the exotic fish, the mouth-brooding African cichlid, Tilapia (*Oreochromis mossambica*). There are other smaller species of tropical American origin, including the guppy (*Poecilia reticulata*) and platy (*Xiphophorus maculatus*), that have naturalised in the hill streams. A number of other exotic fish like trout and carps, introduced for sport and food, have gained the status of vermin locally.

Tilapia is proving to be an invasive vermin that does not spare any of the aquatic habitats throughout the Western Ghats. This species that was first introduced in the reservoirs of India as an edible fish is nurtured by fish-eating people locally and continues to proliferate. Further, as there are only three species of native cichlids (*Etroplus* species) in peninsular India, there is hardly any competition that the Tilapia faces. Of the three species, it is only *Etroplus maculatus* that has a habitat preference and geographical range overlapping with the Tilapia's. This species is much smaller in size and is not a potential native competitor to the invader. *Etroplus suratensis*, although much larger in size than the Tilapia, is a brackish water and estuarine cichlid. *Etroplus canarensis* is a rare endemic cichlid found in south-western Karnataka and northern Kerala. There has been no assessment of the potential risk this little known cichlid faces due to the invasive Tilapia.

Monoculture of teak in wet zones has destroyed the top soil and ground vegetation

The greatest risk of alien invasive species of animals in the Western Ghats is definitely that posed by fish. There is no comprehensive documentation of the number of exotic species of fish that have already naturalised in the streams, rivers, and reservoirs. The South American loricariid catfish (*Plecostomus*) is reported to have escaped into the streams of Kerala. The popular aquarium fish traded as 'sucker' has proved to be a vermin in the streams of North America. There are also other tropical American species of live-bearing fish that have locally invaded the Western Ghats. The common swordtail (*Xiphophorus helleri*) and the mosquito fish (*Gambusia affinis*) are but a couple of examples.

Large-sized non-native catfish belonging to the genera *Pangasius* and *Clarias* are freely traded as food and aquarium species throughout India. Since they closely resemble the native south Indian species, an escape into the wild by these species is not noticed easily. There have also been instances of the predatory tropical American piranhas (*Serrasalmus* species) being deliberately released into the rivers of the Western Ghats. Whether the piranha is already thriving in our waters has not yet been confirmed.

Rivers have also been invaded by many north Indian fishes including some of the major carps like catla, mrigal, and rohu. These fish that were introduced into reservoirs are running wild in the rivers and upstream. These carps are not only hardy and more adaptive, but they also inter-breed with native carps resulting in the emergence of hybrids that have been observed from time to time.

Gardens, monocultures, and human-modified forests have

Forest degradation due to a dam in Valparai

invited many species of urban and agriculture-adapted birds into the Western Ghats. Although the direct impact of ubiquitous species of birds—those without any specialised ecological requirement—on the endemic and habitat specialist species of birds has not been studied, the aggressive habits, omnivorous diets, and the tendency to build up large local populations that species such as crows and mynas (*Acridotheres*) inherently possess can place a lot of demand on the native biodiversity locally.

The south Indian avifauna, which is organised into many habitat-specific communities, is apparently limited by the number of species they can accommodate locally. Although the number of species tends to vary with the different habitats, within the terrestrial bird communities, the number of ecological niches tends to be rather constant. Thus, it is common to see a local insect-eating community of birds consisting of sunbirds, babblers, bulbuls, wood shrikes (and minivets), orioles, iora, woodpeckers, flycatchers, drongos, etc. What is however interesting is the way in which the closely related species of birds, which belong to one or more of the families to which the insect-eating birds belong, replace each other with slight changes in the habitat and local ecological conditions in the Western Ghats. For example, within heterogeneous landscapes, as the habitats shift from village-agriculture through secondary forests to mature rainforests, one can observe the red-vented bulbul and the white-browed bulbuls give way to the red-whiskered and ruby-throated bulbuls and also to the grey-headed, yellow-browed and black bulbuls. Similar examples can be seen amongst woodpeckers, babblers and other insect-eating birds.

It is fortunate that no species of birds in Western Ghats has earned the rather unpopular reputation of a 'vermin'. It is nevertheless likely that a handful of species would soon be branded as vermin—potential candidates being the house crow (*Corvus splendens*), Indian myna (*Acridotheres tristis*), and rose-ringed parakeet (*Psittacula krameri*). The rapid and local loss of forests and the spread of townships have together created ideal habitats for some of these ubiquitous birds. Although the crow can shift between being a predator and a scavenger, the myna and parakeets aggressively compete for nest-holes with most of the other hole-nesting birds.

Many species of mammals have earned the unfortunate status of vermin in the Western Ghats. House rats (*Rattus rattus*) have invaded even the *shola* forests. The field rat (*Millardia meltada*), which is a pest throughout the plains of India, has invaded the highest grasslands in the Nilgiri Hills. Newly created habitats and unintentional introductions by humans have favoured the spread of the three-striped palm squirrel (*Funambulus palmarum*). Bonnet macaque (*Macaca radiata*) is yet another species of mammal that has proliferated locally, thanks to the many pilgrim centres, tourist spots and roadside temples providing food and protection. Decimation of the population of predators has also favoured the proliferation of the wild boar (*Sus scrofa*). Wild boars can place a lot of pressure on plants, with underground tubers and fallen fruits interfering with forest regeneration. They also devour terrestrial animals, including frogs, especially when they emerge in large numbers.

Dry forests are highly prone to fire during summer

Feral dogs, cats, cattle, and buffaloes are a common feature throughout the Western Ghats. Dogs and cats prey on birds and small mammals inside forests near human habitations. Dogs compete with the larger carnivores by sneaking on their kills. Feral cattle and buffaloes not only compete with the other herbivores for fodder and water but are also responsible for the spread of epidemics including the dreaded foot-and-mouth disease.

Cattle that Devour

Cattle probably first entered the Western Ghats with the Todas. Buffaloes must have come in later as the pastoral communities found them hardier in the wet regions and more capable of defending themselves against the larger predators like the leopard and tiger. The large numbers of cattle (including buffaloes) that freely graze and move through the forests from time to time are the biggest non-human threat to biodiversity. Free-ranging cattle trample forest floor, seeds and saplings, and destroy them. They even graze in the higher hills where the endangered and endemic Nilgiri tahr (*Hemitragus hylocrius*) precariously survives.

A family of nomads and their pets on the move through Ulttara Kannada

Starved and free-ranging domestic cattle place a heavy demand on the forests and grasslands throughout the Western Ghats. Masinagudi, for instance, the mainstay of cattle in the Nilgiri Hills has about fifteen thousand in number. Ten thousand tonnes of cow dung used to be removed from this area for commercial purposes. These cattle freely graze within the Mudumalai Wildlife Sanctuary, competing with the wild herbivores. A crude estimate suggests that the daily removal of natural biomass by these cattle would amount to one hundred tonnes or twelve lorry loads, considering the daily food intake of an average bovine to be at least five kilogrammes.

The need to create fresh and green pastures for the cattle has driven the local populace to periodically set fire to forests and grasslands. And when these cattle wander into protected areas that are dedicated to tigers and other carnivores, they get killed, leading to conflicts between humans and the predators. Such conflicts invariably result in the loss of predators, even tigers, as the agitated people resort to any means including the use of deadly poisons in eliminating the killers. Poisoning the carcasses of cattle and leaving them out in the forests has led to the death of both adult and young tigers. Sometimes, bears, porcupines and other scavenging mammals also tend to get poisoned accidently if they visit these carcasses.

Feral buffaloes are widespread in the southern Western Ghats. They are quite common along the Moyar River in and around the Nilgiri hills. Smaller populations are also seen in the southernmost parts, especially in the hills of Kanyakumari district. These aggressive feral buffaloes have completely adapted to the region, quite resembling the wild water buffalo. They are large and have the potential of competing with the gaur for food and habitat. Unlike the native gaur, the feral buffaloes are intolerant of humans and would not hesitate to attack people who stray closer. Till a majority of the buffaloes were killed by an epidemic outbreak of suspected foot-and-mouth disease in the early 1980s, they had also placed a lot of grazing pressure on the high altitude grasslands that were home to the Nilgiri tahr.

How exactly the feral buffaloes got established in the Western Ghats continues to remain a mystery. The Todas probably were

Photo: R Prabhakar

the first to have brought them in. Toda buffaloes presumably ran free from settlements and spread in the region. Oral history, however, suggests that the Todas released the buffaloes into the forests as part of a 'living sacrifice'. According to local informants, the Toda would dedicate buffaloes born on Fridays to the gods and set them free in the forest after weaning.

There are also suggestions that they moved in much later along with the pastoral Gowlis of the northern Western Ghats. In the Kanyakumari district, it is believed that the feral buffaloes are the descendents of a domestic stock that a local herder abandoned in recent times. It is quite likely that all theories are probable. The buffalo, which, unlike the domesticated cattle, still retains its ancestral taxonomic identity and characteristics could have easily adapted to the local conditions once set free. Populations, thus, got established under different circumstances locally. Suggestions that the buffalo is native to the Western Ghats have been dismissed by wildlife biologists. Also, the pressure that feral buffaloes place on the habitats of the native gaur (and other grazers) has not yet been assessed.

Man and Beast in Conflict

There have been various kinds of conflicts between humans and animals in the Western Ghats over the ages. Historical accounts of the Exodus of Hebrews out of Egypt led by Moses provided in the

A buffalo crèche in Masingudi

Old Testament describe outbreaks of locusts and frogs as pestilences. While locust-human conflict is still a major concern in many parts of the world especially in Africa, frogs as 'pestilence' is not quite well-known. In the historical account of Moses, it is said that God brought frogs in the millions out of the river Nile to punish the Pharoah and his people. The frogs spread everywhere in the Pharoah's land and when they died, the entire kingdom stank!

Frogs 'punishing' people sounds quite absurd, yet it seems to be happening even today. Thariyode and Padinjerathara, two villages adjoining the Kuttitadi dam in Wayanad district of Kerala, reported the mass emergence of the bi-coloured frog (*Rana curtipes*) during the months of March and April in 2006. Villagers witnessed millions of freshly metamorphosed bi-coloured frogs that swarmed homes, courtyards, gardens, and roads. Unable to prevent it from getting into kitchens, cooking vessels, and other domestic nooks and crannies, the frenzied villagers apparently resorted to killing the frogs using bleaching powder. Elsewhere, thousands of migrating frogs were left on the roads, dead and stinking, crushed under the wheels of vehicles and rendering the villagers in a state of panic fearing an imminent outbreak of epidemic disease.

Lowland wetlands in Mudumalai WLS called 'Vayal' are largely under rice cultivation

The entire event took a dramatic turn as it happened around the time when the people of Kerala were preparing for the polls. The agitated villagers, the press, as well as the public at large considered the swarm of frogs as a 'pestilence' and accused the government for their lack of concern. In fact, people in Thariyode and

Padinjerathara had even declared that they would boycott polling as a mark of resentment towards the government's 'indifference'.

The panic caused by the emerging and migrating baby frogs is entirely due to the lack of awareness amongst the local inhabitants supplemented by the apathy of the wildlife biologists and naturalists. Mass emergence of the bi-coloured frog after complete metamorphosis is not unusual. Such mass emergence (or migration) has been observed from time to time in the Moyar River and Thekkady reservoir, and probably even in Shimoga. In Thekkady, one such outburst in the 1970s had apparently attracted a number of wild boars that feasted on the baby frogs.

The bi-coloured frog is endemic, has the largest tadpoles in the country, and completes its aquatic larval life in streams and reservoirs. The large tadpoles move about like schools of fish and emerge on land *en masse*. Nothing is known about the significance of the tadpole-size and schooling behaviour and far less has been understood about the survival rates of the frogs after metamorphosis. The recent episode reported from the village in Kerala could be an exceptionally large local recruitment, probably triggered by the abundant rains during 2005.

Conflicts between people and snakes form some of the earliest examples of man against beast contests. Many species of larger snakes, especially the rock python (*Python molurus*) and king cobra, have declined drastically in number or perished locally due to wanton killing. The other reptile that has suffered seriously at the hands of men is the marsh crocodile or mugger (*Crocodylus palustris*). The mugger that was found in almost all rivers in the Western Ghats till recently has been slowly decimated. Today the single largest population is found in the Moyar River in Tamil Nadu. Other local populations are largely confined to the reservoirs where they are directly protected by the State Forest Departments.

Birds, too, that visit the cultivated areas have suffered extensive persecution at the hands of local farmers. They have fallen prey to the pesticides being used if not directly being shot and killed. To scare birds out of the fields, various devices have also been ingeniously developed by farmers. When a species of bird has been identified as a threat to crops, farmers do not hesitate to destroy their nests. The common weaverbird (*Ploceus philippensis*) is often the unfortunate victim. Birds of prey that lift chicken are trapped and killed, or are brought down with stones or bullets. Peafowl that raid crops are simply poisoned to death. Night birds, including the hawk cuckoo and scops owl, are locally considered as bad omen. People do not hesitate to kill these birds if they decided to stay within the neighbourhood and sing!

The worst form of human-animal conflict has for years been between mammals and people. Even small mammals like rodents and bats have shared a hostile relationship with humans. Bats and squirrels (especially flying squirrels) that visit orchards are killed. Even monkeys are not spared. All small carnivores are seen as pests as they venture to steal chicken, other domestic birds and small mammals. Wild boar is a major source of conflict in farms bordering forests. Jackals, too, are perceived as destructive to sugarcane. No one tolerates the *dhole* (wild dog). Local humans may even harass the *dhole* to part with its kill.

Man-eating leopards and tigers and rogue elephants have been reasons for the wanton killing of these species throughout the past, although poaching for skin and tusks has been the most serious form of human pressure on these mammals. Relentless killings still continue. Leopards and tigers that prey on cattle are promptly killed by using poisoned baits. Elephants that stray into cultivated areas are either shot or electrocuted. The latter practice is now widely prevalent.

Ironically, in the Western Ghats, like most other places, the animals that are the most in conflict with humans are those that are also 'sacred'. Let us take the elephant for example. People living in the northern Western Ghats are all devotees of Lord Ganesha—the elephant god. Year after year, the Ganesha festival is celebrated with a lot of devotion and ostentation. Yet, the elephant has largely been eliminated in the region.

What of the tiger? Many temples in the northern Western Ghats have been dedicated to the tiger. *Hulathervaru* means the 'tiger god' in the Western Ghats of Karnataka. Much like elephants, tigers have also perished in the north. But for the tiger reserves in the south, the large cat would have been totally eliminated in this region.

Cashew cultivation in coastal landscapes

Other sacred animals in conflict with humans locally are the bonnet macaque, common langur, peafowl, and cobra. Why does this happen? Is this a historical trend or is it due to the recent changes in local cultures, attitudes, and traditions induced by immigration and development? Or is it some early wisdom that foresaw the extinction of these animals and gave them the conservation status of being sacred?

The Survivors

Despite the various forms of human concerns and outcry regarding loss of biodiversity and habitats, few species of animals have definitely gone extinct in the Western Ghats. With the possible exception of the Malabar civet, confirmed extinctions have only been local. Local extinctions have led to the disappearance of the elephant from most of its historical range. Tigers, too, have been rendered scarce. The endemic mammals like the lion-tailed macaque (LTM), the Nilgiri langur, and the Nilgiri tahr are in such low numbers that their continued survival is today a matter of worldwide concern. The single largest population of the mugger (marsh crocodile) is in the Moyar River, where about ten years ago its population was estimated to be three hundred.

The lion-tailed macaque is one of the few carefully studied mammals in the Western Ghats. In 1985, the population of this primate in the state of Karnataka was estimated as three thousand. More recent estimates have placed the numbers in Karnataka between one thousand and two thousand. A smaller population is known to exist in Tamil Nadu. Including the nearly two thousand individuals in Kerala, the population of LTM has been most recently placed at four thousand. LTM is primarily an inhabitant of evergreen rainforests below seven hundred metres ASL, with a home range of 1.25 square kilometres. How long can the Western Ghats sustain this species? Although there are no predictions available, it does seem that the LTM population is gradually growing. With better protection of both the primate and its preferred habitats, local populations are apparently doing well. Sizeable numbers of LTM have been observed in habitats and locations that were not earlier known. If re-assessed, it may well be found that the total population of LTM in the Western Ghats has exceeded the earlier estimate of four thousand.

A clean and tidy settlement within Mudumalai WLS

The Nilgiri tahr exists in the higher elevations between Nilgiri Hills and Ashambu Hills. Over this 400-kilometre range, not more than two thousand animals have been estimated to occur—150 (Nilgiri Hills), 570–690 (Anaimalai Hills), 890 (Eravikulam), 280–310 (Palani hills), and a handful over the rest of the range. Despite a regime of strict protection, the Nilgiri tahr population is not improving. As such, the question remains, 'Is there adequate habitat for the species?'

Smaller populations of the tahr that inhabit the precipitous slopes have been spared outside the ranges exclusively dedicated for the conservation of the species. In the hill ranges of Kerala that surround the Periyar Tiger Reserve, the tahr habitat is also the home of the endemic and rare palm *Bentinckia codapanna*. The association between the palm and the tahr may have been a more widespread one during the past. Does the local disappearance of the already threatened palm signal the erosion of Nilgiri tahr in the Western Ghats?

Poaching continues to take a toll on the Nilgiri tahr. Poachers devise ingenious methods to eliminate the tahr without the use of guns and traps. Banana leaves smeared with oil or grease and placed along the trails of the tahr make them slip and fall to death as they leap from ledge to ledge. There may be other such gruesome ways in which the tahr gets poached from time to time. Apparently, stones, clubs and dogs are also used to hunt the tahr that stray out of their natural habitat. Local inhabitants are able to lure the tahr within reach by burning grass and inducing fresh growth that the younger animals are unable to resist.

The elephant is another species of endangered mammal that has attracted both scientific and popular interest. Recent estimates place the population of elephants in the states of Karnataka, Tamil Nadu, and Kerala at 12,500. A majority of this population is within protected areas. Unlike the LTM, the elephant is more of a habitat generalist, utilising a wide range of natural and man-made habitats in and around the Western Ghats. This habit makes the elephant vulnerable to poaching as it tends to stray into cultivation and estates.

Historically, the elephants have used a number of corridors for their movement in the Western Ghats. These well-used corridors also linked the Western Ghats with the neighbouring

Eastern Ghats and other parts of the Deccan plateau in peninsular India. Many of the corridors have unfortunately been blocked by recent development which includes the construction of dams and roads, establishment of estates and human settlements etc. Independent studies have proved beyond doubt that the encroachment of the corridors has been the primary cause of human-elephant conflicts in the Western Ghats.

The tiger has been comparatively better studied amongst the large carnivores in the Western Ghats. It is presently restricted to the states of Karnataka, Kerala, and Tamil Nadu, though an occasional adult may stray into Maharashtra. The exact status of the population of this large and elusive cat is much less predictable than that of the elephant, Nilgiri tahr or LTM; estimates have placed the number of tigers from four hundred to six hunderd. Research on the natural food habits of larger carnivores in Nagarhole has suggested that the tiger selectively preys on animals weighing more than 176 kilogrammes. Non-selective predation by the tiger is more likely the result of prey scarcity.

Elephants retreating into the forests after a drink in Mudumalai

The considerable debate around the 'best' method of assessment has made it difficult to accept suggestions that the tiger population has shown an increasing trend since the Project Tiger was first launched. Scarcity of appropriate prey animals is the primary factor that leads a tiger to kill cattle. Cattle-lifting in turn leads to human-tiger conflicts where the beast is invariably the loser. The future of the tiger is indeed bleak, especially in view of the fact that its prey-base is not being conserved with the same rigour and there is little chance of its survival outside the strictly protected reserves. There are also indications of poachers having set eye their eyes on the Western Ghats in view of the tiger population in central and northern India declining.

Constrained by Development

Soon after the British took over the forests and wildlife, restrictions were imposed on the traditional use of forestlands. In 1848, shifting cultivation was put under regulations. By 1860, the Government of Madras had banned shifting cultivation. Following these restrictions on traditional land use systems, the grazing rights of the hill-dwellers in the Western Ghats were curbed. Soon, the Cattle Trespassing Act (1871) came into existence. Forests were brought under the management of the State and the system of 'reserved' forests established.

The British conservation efforts first began by way of targeting species of plant, the best example in the Western Ghats being the tali palm (*Corypha umbraculifera*). The Kumri Marati community and other forest-dwelling human communities use the starchy core of the palm as a supplement during seasons of lean food availability while the large fan-like leaves are also used as thatch. This monocarpic palm—a plant that flowers only once, sets seeds, and dies—does not have a succession of different aged recruits that ensures a continuous supply of starch for the people who depend on it. As a result, the wild population tends to get enriched locally by forest-dwelling people who seed and nurture it within patches of secondary rainforests. Consequently, we find certain landscapes being locally dominated by the palm. It is hence remarkable that the Forest Department in the Uttara Kannada district,

Makeshift watch-posts as this one are common wherever wild animals tend to raid crops

where the largest population of the tali palm is found at present, drafted an exclusive working plan—'No. 10: Honnavar Tali Palm Forest Working Plan, 1906'—to conserve the palm.

Although the British declared large areas of forests as 'reserved' for different purposes, including felling of timber trees and hunting for sport, efforts to systematically bring vast areas of forests under a system of Protected Areas (PAs) were not in place till the Wildlife Protection Act (1972), came into force. Since then, a total area of 14,140.36 square kilometres has been brought under the system of PA in the Western Ghats alone. The PA network, which includes two biosphere reserves (Nilgiri and Agasthiyamalai), thirteen national parks (NP) and forty-six wildlife sanctuaries (WLS), together amounts to a mere 8.8 percent of the Western Ghats. (*see table 13*) Of these, Bandipur, Periyar and Kalakad-Mundanthurai were designated as Project Tiger Reserves. A fourth tiger reserve has been recently proposed by the Government of Kerala and will include the Parambikulam and Chinnar Wildlife Sanctuaries and a part of the Indira Gandhi Wildlife Sanctuary in Tamil Nadu.

Ninety-one percent of the Western Ghats is under pressure from various forms of development. These pressures are virtually choking the nearly sixty PAs, threatening plant and animal communities that have enjoyed some protection during the past. The population of tigers that recovered rather dramatically since the launch of the Project Tiger has since been under threat as they

The narrow coastline that characterises Uttara Kannada and Goa

Table 13: Distribution of PAs in the Western Ghats

State	PAs		Area (sq. kms.)	Status
Gujarat	1.	Bansda (Vansda)	23.99	NP
	2.	Purna	160.84	WLS
Maharashtra	3.	Sanjay Gandhi (Borivili)	86.96	NP
	4.	Kalsubai	361.71	WLS
	5.	Tansa	304.81	WLS
	6.	Bhimashankar	130.78	WLS
	7.	Chandoli	308.97	WLS
	8.	Karnala	4.48	WLS
	9.	Koyna	423.55	WLS
	10.	Phansad	69.79	WLS
	11.	Rhadanagiri	351.16	WLS
	12.	Sarageshwar	10.87	WLS
Goa	13.	Molem	107.00	NP
	14.	Bondla	8.00	WLS
	15.	Cotigao	85.65	WLS
	16.	Madei	208.00	WLS
	17.	Molem	133.00	WLS
	18.	Netravalli	211.00	WLS
Karnataka	19.	Kudremukh	600.32	NP
	20.	Nagarhole	643.39	NP*
	21.	Bandipur	874.00	NP*
	22.	Anshi	250.00	NP
	23.	Bhadra	492.46	WLS
	24.	BRT Hills	539.52	WLS
	25.	Brahmagiri	181.29	WLS
	26.	Dandeli	843.16	WLS
	27.	Ghataprabha	29.78	WLS
	28.	Gudavi	0.73	WLS
	29.	Mookambika	247.00	WLS
	30.	Nugu	30.32	WLS*
	31.	Pushpagiri	102.92	WLS
	32.	Sharavathi Valley	431.23	WLS
	33.	Shettihalli	395.60	WLS
	34.	Someshwara	88.40	WLS
	35.	Talakaveri	105.59	WLS
Tamil Nadu	36.	Indira Gandhi	117.10	NP*
	37.	Mudumalai	103.24	NP*
	38.	Mukurti	78.46	NP*
	39.	Indira Gandhi	841.49	WLS*
	40.	Kalakkad	223.58	WLS
	41.	Mudumalai	217.36	WLS*
	42.	Mundanthurai	567.38	WLS
	43.	Sriviliputtur	465.20	WLS
	44.	Kanyakumari	-	WLS
Kerala	45.	Silent Valley	89.52	NP*
	46.	Eravikulam	97.00	NP
	47.	Periyar	350.00	NP*
	48.	Aralam	55.00	WLS

49.	Chimmony	90.00	WLS*
50.	Chinnar	90.44	WLS*
51.	Idukki	70.00	WLS*
52.	Neyyar	128.00	WLS
53.	Parambikulam	285.00	WLS*
54.	Peechi-Vazhani	125.00	WLS
55.	Peppara	53.00	WLS
56.	Periyar	777.00	WLS*
57.	Shendurney	100.32	WLS
58.	Thattekadu	21.16	WLS
59.	Wayanad	344.44	WLS

Note: Asterisk indicates those PAs that are in part or full declared as Project Elephant Reserves.

tend to stray out of the PAs from time to time. Of the ten Project Elephant Reserves that have been identified in the country, four are in the Western Ghats. The majority of the 12,500 elephants that are estimated to be present in the region are largely confined to the reserves in Tamil Nadu and Kerala. (*see table 14*)

The rate at which development impacts the Western Ghats may soon limit the natural forests and associated biodiversity to the nearly nine percent of land that lies within the PA network. The 160,000 square kilometres region that encompasses the Western Ghats is currently divided into not less than forty-five districts—three in Gujarat, eleven in Maharashtra, two in Goa, ten in Karnataka, fourteen in Kerala and seven in Tamil Nadu. The

Table 14: Project Elephant Reserves Identified and the Estimated Elephant Populations in the Western Ghats

Reserve	Area (sq. kms.)	Elephant population
Nilgiri Hills-Eastern Ghats	11,000-12,000	5,000-6,300
Nilambur-Silent Valley-Coimbatore	2,500	500-956
Anaimalai-Parambikulam	3,000-5,700	1,000-1,600
Periyar	3,000	1,500-2,000
Total	**19,500-23,200**	**8,000-10,586**

Note: The estimates of elephant populations provided by the Asian Elephant Research and Conservation Centre, and Wildlife Institute of India vary considerably. About 6,000 square kilometres of these reserves actually fall outside the limits of the Western Ghats despite being contiguous. An estimated 682–2,100 elephants occur in these areas.

density of human population within these eight districts varies from less than two hundred per square kilometre (Dangs in Gujarat; Dhule and Sindudurga in Maharashtra; Uttara Kannada, Shimoga, Chikmagalur, Kodagu and Chamrajnagar in Karnataka) to more than one thousand per square kilometre (six districts). One-third of the districts that encompass the Western Ghats have a human population density between two hundred and four hundred per square kilometre. The highest human population density in the Western Ghats region lies within Allapuzha district (1,489 per square kilometre) followed by Trivandrum district (1,476 square kilometre) and Kozhikode district (1,228 square kilometre).

With an average human population density of around five hundred per square kilometre, the region that encompasses the Western Ghats is certainly constrained by the tremendous pressure of development. At the present population density, the per capita land available works out to be 0.2 hectares (around 0.5 acres). Considering the nine percent of land that is held within the system of PAs and the land that is locked under water within dam sites, river valleys, and lakes, it may well turn out that even the estimated per capita land availability of 0.2 hectares is an over-estimate. So clearly, the pressure on land for human development is going to be rather intensive in the years to come.

Naruthi stream — a sacred spot venerated by the inhabitants of Mudumalai WLS

Human development in the Western Ghats has come in many guises, mostly from cattle herders. Independent analyses of threats to the region have all pointed to the enormous pressure placed by cattle on the pristine landscapes. Added to the mounting pressure on land, the need (both domestic and market-driven) for naturally growing plant biomass—fodder, fuel, fibre, furniture, food, and medicine—has placed unforeseen pressure on most landscapes in the Western Ghats. And as the soil and water resources within the private holdings and common lands are rapidly eroding due to bad practices and over-use, the demand to denotify reserved forests and PAs is on the rise.

The unresolved dispute over water-sharing between the states has forced the government to build newer dams or fortify the existing ones to enhance their holding capacities. The best example of this is the Mullai-Periyar Dam dispute between Tamil Nadu and Kerala.

A traditional Keralite temple in Periyar

The worst of the water crisis induced development proposals is that of inter-linking rivers. The ecological and social dangers of linking rivers have been pointed out several times. Nevertheless, every time a well-placed government engineer or a political leader is given the public ear, the person does not hesitate to announce his or her intention to link rivers across the region. Thariyode-Padinjerathara or 'frog pestilence' in Kerala is the result of the newly constructed Kuttiyadi dam. While dams do kill a range of land plants and animals by submerging them, they do favour the outbursts of certain invasive species of fish in the local population. And as the rather unusual 'frog pestilence' has brought to notice, a range of dam-induced pestilences in the Western Ghats may not be a far-fetched possibility.

Under these circumstances, the last of the Western Ghats' biodiversity, especially the 'wildlife', will have to be managed within the less than sixty PAs. With little scope of increasing the overall extent of the PA network, coupled with government slackness in implementing other systems of participatory natural resource management such as Ecologically Sensitive Areas (under the Environment Protection Act, 1986), and the twenty-year-long indifference in properly managing the Biosphere Reserves in the region, the life history of wild animals that require larger home ranges and have a tendency to wander will be severely constrained. What most biologists foresee is a situation where wildlife will be found only within PAs, which will eventually function no better than glorified zoos.

Landscape ecologists have often drawn attention to the dynamics of habitats and living communities. They describe what is known as 'shifting mosaics'. Shifting mosaics simply mean that habitats and living communities can never be confined within boundaries as that drawn around a PA or an administrative-political unit as a district, state or country. For instance, patches of rainforests that once occurred within a specified boundary may over the years shrink further or even merge and spill out, entirely changing the structure of the landscape. The shifting vegetation and habitats take along with them the associated plant and animal communities. Rigid administrative or political boundaries are thus a major hindrance to the sustenance of dynamic landscapes—most landscapes indeed being dynamic. Worse still is the concern raised by expert predictions regarding the changing patterns in world climate. Around seventy-five to eighty percent of India's protected forests are likely to change in structure within the next twenty-five to thirty years. Can anyone predict the fate of the Western Ghats' forests currently being constrained within the PA network due to the ever-increasing pressures of human advancement?

Still waters in higher elevations are often home to the introduced trout

Looking Ahead

What's on the Horizon?

Less than nine percent of the Western Ghats enjoy strict protection under the system of Protected Areas (PAs). These PAs are, however, not fully representative of the various vegetation types of the landscape. They are also inadequate in conserving the many endemic species of trees, amphibians, and small mammals. The rainforests are less protected compared to the deciduous forests since the PA system mainly focussed on large mammals. Since the deciduous forests are mostly preferred by large mammals, and much of the hardwood comes from these otherwise less diverse forest types, deciduous forests have traditionally enjoyed greater protection within the system of PAs than the rainforests. Furthermore, a number of forest landscapes that have traditionally enjoyed the status of PAs were only meant to buffer the many reservoirs built in the region. There was no focus on the representativeness of the vegetation and biodiversity of the landscape when a certain area was declared as a PA. As such, the presence of most wildlife (or biodiversity in general) within the *ad hoc* PAs is only incidental.

The rainforests of the Western Ghats are quite mature. Historically, the only landscape that was specifically excluded from being destroyed for the sake of its pristine and species-rich rainforests is the Silent Valley National Park. At least forty-two species of endemic plants were discovered for the first time in Silent Valley. The Silent Valley National Park has served as an eye-opener to natural resource managers and conservationists alike, and the current focus has been on bringing more rainforests within the system of PAs in the Western Ghats. Some of the rainforests, which have great conservation value but are still not within the system of PAs, and are presently 'Reserve Forests', include Kulathapuzha, Palode (Agasthyamalai), Ranni and Konni (Periyar) forests to the west of Eravikulam National Park, south-western Palani Hills, New Amarambalam, forests between Coonoor and Mukurti NPs, forests between Nilambur and Brahmagiri WLSs, Kerti and Pattighat (Kodagu), Gundia, Agumbe and Balahalli (Malnad), Bhimagad, Amboli, and Mahabaleshwar (Maharashtra).

Excellent stands of mature rainforests with dense canopy cover are still seen in the Periyar Tiger Reserve (Kerala) and the adjoining Meghamalai and High Wavy Mountains (Tamil Nadu). A lot of these forests are still outside the regime of PAs. Estimates of standing biomass in the rainforests of Karnataka have suggested that the 478.82 tonnes per hectare is on the higher side when compared with the 233–560 tonnes per hectare that is known in other tropical rainforests. However, the lower primary productivity of 7.7–11.7 tonnes per hectare per year (as against 13–32 tonnes per hectare per year in other tropical rainforests) and leaf litter of 3.277 tonnes per hectare per year (compared to 3–11.9

A leafless African tulip tree reaches out from the Anaimalai Hills

tonnes per hectare per year elsewhere) in the Western Ghats are indications that the forests are slow-growing and may take much longer than tropical rainforests elsewhere in the world to regenerate. Degeneration of rainforests is unfortunately taking place rather rapidly allowing little time for the forests to regenerate and fully recover even under strict protection, especially in the northern landscapes where the dry season lasts for more than five months.

Ecosystem-human combat in the Western Ghats was triggered on a rather large and extended scale probably for the first time in the war that was waged against malaria. While

Montane grasslands are vulnerable to climatic change

inorganic poisons such as DDT were widely dumped without any foresight, parallel efforts were made to 'tame' the ecosystem by planting eucalyptus trees and draining the marshes where the mosquitoes supposedly bred. And after it was realised that the more dangerous species of mosquitoes are those that breed in water collected within tree-holes and that denser canopy made it more conducive for the mosquitoes to breed, rainforests were cleared or thinned out to encourage light penetration and local desiccation.

Against this backdrop, the future scenario in the Western Ghats may be described as follows—one, a degenerate tropical ecosystem with a possible increase in arthropod parasites and vectors such as ticks that transmit diseases like the Kesavanur forest disease (monkey fever) and *Aedes* mosquitoes that spread chickungunya and dengue amongst humans locally; two, diseases carried around by humans and their livestock (such as foot-and-mouth disease and the most recent H5N1 strain of the bird flu) that may take a heavy toll of wild animals, and three, a marked increase in light-tolerant species of plants and animals that are quite adaptable to the continuous ecological disturbances that are induced by development. Since the three likely situations are also inter-linked, they can work in synergy to create rather complex and unforeseen ecological disasters.

Recent studies in the forests of Mudumalai that have experienced intense pressures from human beings as well as cattle have suggested that the largest of the remaining trees are likely to be *Ficus*. Trees that have utility value both for the local human community and mammals like the elephant do not survive to grow to their maximum girth and height. Localised plant communities such as Myristica swamps tend to disappear with the fragmentation of the rainforests. Plants with specialised breeding systems are likely to become rarer due to their low densities. Over-exploitation of certain herbs might lead to local extinctions, endangering other organisms that exclusively depend on them, such as some species of endemic butterflies.

Many endemic species of fish inhabit the fast-flowing, clear, and well-aerated waters of the Western Ghats. The muddy waters, created by land erosion and pollution, will encourage the predominance of fish that are adapted to oxygen-deficient water. Further, the proposed inter-linking of rivers will only hasten the spread of invasive species such as the Tilapia. Somewhat sedentary animals such as amphibians, reptiles, birds (like the laughing thrushes and forest babblers), and arboreal mammals will suffer a greater population fragmentation.

The Western Ghats are not yet fully explored. Several new species are being described, both plants and animals, with the probable exception of butterflies, birds, and mammals. New species of bryophytes are being found in the region. In the Kalakad-Mundanthurai Tiger Reserve alone, nineteen species of flowering plants have been identified for the first time in recent years. Freshwater fishes are being added to the existing list quite frequently. However, it is the series of new amphibian species discovered in the recent years, and the supposed lot that awaits taxonomic description, that has suddenly created a flutter amongst field biologists.

Mahonia—an ice age relic

More species of amphibians have been described for the first time in the past fifteen years than any other group of vertebrate animals. While it is remarkable that such diversity is not seen in other groups of vertebrates, a rush for finding and describing new species of amphibians in Western Ghats is proving to be a dangerous trend. Amateur and professional biologists who spend time in the forests of the Western Ghats are constantly collecting specimens of amphibians in the hope of finding 'new' species.

Amphibians are polymorphic, as expected amongst animals that are food to a large number of other animals. Frogs that live amongst leaves in grass, bushes and the tree canopy are most vulnerable to predation by birds and other animals. Hence, they are bound to vary enormously in colour and other external features. Most species also tend to change colour with age, season, moods, and the background. The great diversity of external characters, particularly colours that are displayed by amphibians in the Western Ghats, has not been fully documented. Amateur biologists are easily perplexed by the great diversity of external characters that these amphibians sport and do not hesitate to collect any individual that looks a little different. Rampant collection of amphibians for taxonomic purposes can potentially threaten amphibian populations locally.

A common streamside damselfly (*Neurobasis chinensis*)

The Nilgiris cricket frog

The calls of frogs and toads play a much greater role in reproductive isolation of biological species than morphological features. There is also a dearth of information on the life history stages of even the more common species. Due to these constraints and lack of attributes like interaction, experience, guidance, and patience amongst the field biologists, there exists a considerable amount of confusion in amphibian taxonomy. Suggestions that such confusion can be minimised by integrating the molecular and other anatomical taxonomical tools with traditional and classical taxonomy, as often proposed, can only lead to further pressures of collecting samples of the already threatened amphibian populations in Western Ghats.

At a time when it is fully acknowledged that the Western Ghats are a hot-spot of biodiversity, and that amphibians (and many other groups of plants and animals) have apparently diversified locally much more than elsewhere in the world, adding many more species to the existing list is not going to further enhance the conservation value of the region. And unless a unified 'Code of Ethics' is developed and adopted by field biologists, collection of specimens can be really damaging to its biodiversity.

Dillenia pentagyna a keystone species; a hot-speck(below)

While taxonomic research is important, what is more critical to conservation planning is a better understanding of how species are organised into living communities and what are the factors that determine the apparent patterns. Patterns of organisation and spatial distribution of animal communities in the Western Ghats are barely understood till now. Factors that influence the structure and spatial distribution of bird communities are far better understood than that of any other class of animals in the region. However, it has been shown that birds can at best be indicators of ecosystem health at scales of large geographical spaces as landscapes.

Environmental impacts that affect living vertebrate communities locally are better understood by changes in the structure of fish, amphibians, and reptiles. Unfortunately, but for a handful of rather local studies, the focus on the lower, cold-blooded vertebrates has largely been taxonomic. Unless the focus on lower vertebrates and other lesser known groups of animals and plants, including invertebrates, ferns, and mosses, is shifted from being totally taxonomic to community-ecological, conservation planning in the Western Ghats will continue to be guided by *ad hoc* recommendations and ghosts of the early British wisdom!

Socio-economic demands on the biodiversity of Western Ghats are likely to increase in the years to come. The current dampening trend in the tea industry has already forced well-established corporates including the multinational Hindustan Lever Limited to part with their estates. Major tea producing landscapes in Kerala and Tamil Nadu wear a deserted look as several other smaller industries have simply abandoned the estates. The result is that the labour force that is unable to subsist outside the tea gardens are locally managing sections of vast estates and trading the produce. Since the returns are far less than what was probably earned through organised labour, the desolate estate workers are placing greater pressure on the adjacent forests to supplement their day to day needs. Of greater concern is the possibility that some of the vast estates that are designated to be sold will be bought by well-placed industrialists with the intention of developing them into tourist and recreation resorts, adding pressure to the already

These ancient rocks that surround Sabarimala tend to appear like the heads of elephants

constrained biodiversity of the ecological hot-spot.

Other multinational companies who have maintained vast estates are beginning to contemplate a shift in cropping from tea to tree-horticulture and agro-forestry. Such a shift in the system of cultivation may be complementary to the traditional coffee and cardamom cultivation in the Western Ghats. The traditional system of coffee and cardamom cultivation in the region favoured the preservation of the rainforests in its mature form for years. Minimal removal of undergrowth to allow the crops to grow retained fairly dense tree-canopy that encouraged communities of animals to thrive within the cultivated landscapes. In parts of Kerala where the shortage of affordable labour has forced the cultivation to be largely neglected, the forests are slowly reverting to their original structure.

While the traditional system of inter-cropping in the forests has locally favoured the diversity of plants and animals within the otherwise human-dominated landscapes, whether the practice will be sustained through the years to come is becoming a serious concern. Firstly, agro-forestry continues to attract exotic trees; coffee-growers (like the tea-planters) are increasingly preferring planting silver oak (*Grevillea robusta*). Secondly, high-yielding coffee and cardamom that can grow without shade are gaining popularity in the Western Ghats. Since such cultivation could permit mechanisation as labour grows dearer, the light-tolerant varieties are likely to replace the shade-loving traditional varieties of cardamom and coffee.

Also, pet trade is likely to place increasing pressure on certain species of spiders (tarantulas), fish, and birds. The culture of living within small high-rise apartments is encouraging city dwellers, both in India and abroad, to choose a range of pets that can be confined to smaller spaces such as aquaria, terraria, and cages. The fancy for giant spiders that do not spin webs has picked up quite rapidly fuelled by television and there is a fair demand for tarantulas even in the Western Ghats. While some of the spiders that are locally trapped and traded, for example, in Parambikulam, get out of the country with the foreign tourists, a few probably stay within the country.

Stream fish from the Western Ghats reached the international aquarium trade more than one hundred years ago. Some like the rosy barb (*Puntius conchonius*) and the zebra danio (*Danio rerio*) have since been domesticated and selectively bred to such an extent that they no longer resemble their wild ancestors. Other species with a long history in international trade include the blue danio (*Danio malabaricus*) and tiger panchax (*Aplocheilus lineatus*). More recently, a number of other species, including endemics such as the melon barb (*Puntius melampyx*), Denison's barb (*Puntius denisonii*), chromide (*Etroplus canarensis*), the Travancore dwarf pufferfish (*Tetraodon travancoricus*) and a number of loaches (*Botia and Nemacheilus*) have joined this list.

Coastal forests are largely replaced by horticulture

The Marine Products Development Authority (MPEDA), which monitors the international trade in aquarium fish, lists more than three hundred species of Indian fish. Of these, a number of species are from the Western Ghats. While the National Bureau of Fish Genetic Resources (NBFGR) launched and supported a number of research projects that focused on the captive breeding of some of the endemic fish that are in trade and a few species like the leaf fish (*Pristolepis marginata*) that have been successfully bred in Kerala, large-scale breeding of ornamental endemic fish that meets the international demand is still a distant dream. In the absence of a proper institutional arrangement that addresses the issue of live fish trade in the Western Ghats, the pressure on the wild population will continue to mount rendering the already rare and endemic species more vulnerable to extinction.

The most popular south Indian bird in international pet trade is probably the hill myna (*Gracula religiosa*). Despite regulations, a small number of hill mynas from the Western Ghats do get into the trade. There is unfortunately very little that is known about the way in which live birds from the Western Ghats hit the domestic and international pet shops. Early pet trade probably wiped out the population of the Alexandrine parakeet (*Psittacula eupatria*) from the southern Western Ghats. Parrots from the Western Ghats, including the endemic Malabar parakeet, show up in local pet markets from time to time though in small numbers. Although live bird trade in the region has not yet emerged as a major threat to biodiversity, it can turn out be a conservation challenge in the years to come, in the absence of proper monitoring. Proposals recommending provisions for artificial nest-boxes to induce the hill myna to breed more than once a year have surfaced quite often from the Indian pet trade sector, and are being presented an ideal model for the sustainable harvesting of a valuable wild species. The potential threat to the biodiversity of Western Ghats posed by the pet industry, therefore, needs to be both specifically and collectively addressed in the coming years.

Hoya—an unusual climber with succulent button-like leaves

Domestic livestock, unless restricted to ranches and stalls, will place a greater demand on forestland and biomass. Unrestrained movement of cattle and buffaloes will lead to more human-wild animal conflicts, especially when a cow or a buffalo gets killed by a

Bunches of small fleshy fruits ae a treat to bulbuls and thrushes

predator. Livestock-centred conflicts between people on one hand, and wildlife and the managers of PAs on the other, will only intensify since domestic animals are being used as 'pawns' in the battle over local land ownership and grazing rights.

The buffalo in its feral form is already spreading across the southern landscapes. There is unfortunately no information on its population size and spread. The grazing habitats of the native bovine herbivores including the gaur, tahr, four-horned antelope and blackbuck are pre-empted by the feral buffaloes and domestic livestock. It is not uncommon to see domestic livestock grazing along with some of these herbivores even within the PAs. Despite the growing awareness about potential dangers posed by livestock as carriers of contagious diseases and parasites in the Western Ghats restricting the movement of cattle, buffaloes, sheep, and goats within and around the wildlife habitats, is a rather sensitive issue—often politically motivated. The recent scheme in Tamil Nadu to provide goats to unemployed rural youth which is still far beyond the horizon is one such populist proposal. In fact, the mounting pressure from the political front to denotify reserved lands and forests for distribution amongst tribals and landless agricultural labour, and the utopian notions guiding apex authorities (such as the Tiger Task Force to say that people can live in 'harmony' with wildlife), have only succeeded in pushing the targets farther and completely out of sight!

Ad hoc decisions by the government to open up the Western Ghats in order to locally rehabilitate Sri Lankan Tamil repatriates in Tamil Nadu and Tibetan refugees in Karnataka continue to attract criticism from not only the conservationists but also the general public. Since the south Indian tea industry is going through a major crisis and is closer to a probable collapse, the Tamil Nadu government is forced to sustain the TANTEA infrastructure by spending a good deal of money that is annually earmarked for forest development. The TANTEA that was established as a special wing of the Tamil Nadu Forest Department, primarily to create employment opportunities for the Sri Lankan Tamils in the Western Ghats, is just one amongst the many long-term government schemes that are crying for attention in the region.

Many serious concerns about the future of the Western Ghats have cast their shadows on the horizon. Despite the rather committed efforts made by a large number of people in the country in outlining a National Biodiversity Strategy and Action Plan (NBSAP), the Ministry of Environment and Forests of the Government of India has decided to disown it. It now seems that the information on India's biodiversity and people put together by this nationwide exercise and the road maps drawn for reaching the various goals outlined in the Convention on Biological Diversity merit only academic worth and would only end up in some archive. With the rejection of the NBSAP, regional plans such as those for the Western Ghats have also lost their relevance. Nevertheless, at least one of the recommendations from the 'NBSAP–Western Ghats Eco-region' has successfully drawn attention to the need for the establishment of a Western Ghats Conservation Planning and Development Board (WGCPDB).

The need for a statutory body such as the WGCPDB was first highlighted in 1988. A seminar on 'Conservation and Ecological

The tahr habitat bordering Periyar Tiger Reserve

Secondary forests   A coral tree in bloom

Management of the Western Ghats through Land-use Planning' was organised by the Palni Hills Conservation Council (PHCC) in Kodaikanal. The seminar that was well-attended by activists and experts recommended that all state governments should be urged to set up statutorily constituted WGCPDBs with full administrative and financial responsibility as early as possible, preferably within the year 1988 itself, and empowered to issue ordinances.

'NBSAP–Western Ghats Eco-region' has only reiterated the recommendations of PHCC with a slight difference—instead of each state constituting an exclusive Board, there could be a regional WGCPDB with all the states as members, and with the following mandate:

- The Board would be non-political with its members drawn through formal invitations and nominations from various government authorities, departments and institutions that concern the Western Ghats—research and academic organisations (including universities), NGOs, and individual activists;
- The members may resolve to elect a set of office-bearers such as the Chairperson or President and a Secretary for effective functioning, whose tenures would be rotational, and the duration of which would be decided by mutual consent;
- The Board would be vested with the authority to examine and approve/modify/reject any project proposal or activity, including 'Impact Assessment Reports', undertaken by any

sector (private, government or others) that has a potentially adverse effect on the Western Ghats;
- The Board would adopt an open and participatory process, drawing upon the wisdom and expertise of not only the members, but also other individuals and institutions of repute and proven expertise;
- The Board would coordinate and oversee the effective implementation of NBSAP–Western Ghats ecological-region.

Although the Board is not yet in place, the suggestion that there should be a better coordination of research and development in the Western Ghats was taken seriously by a number of agencies and individuals, leading to the launch of a 'Western Ghats Forum' (WGF) in 2002. WGF is meant to be a platform for closer interaction amongst all those who are concerned with the future of biodiversity, people, and ecology of the Western Ghats. It is a collective voice that loudly lauds successful actions and mourns the gross neglect and deterioration, be it in research or development. It is our sincere hope that the WGF will strive to integrate science with management in the Western Ghats, without losing sight of the need to improve the quality of life of the people.

Tall trees characterise the rainforests of KMTR

Sources of Information

Ali, S. and Ripley, S. D. (1983) *Handbook of the Birds of India and Pakistan* (compact edition). New Delhi, Oxford University Press.

Ali, T M M and Ganeshaiah, K N (1998) *Current Science* 75(3): 201-204.

Ambrose, D P (2003) Biodiversity of Indian Assassin Bugs (Insecta: Hemiptera: Reduviidae) In: ENVIS Bulletin Vol 4(1): *Wildlife and Protected Areas, Conservation of Rainforests in India* (ed) A K Gupta, Ajith Kumar and V Ramakantha: 229-242.

Ambrose, D P and Raj, S (2005) Zoo's Print Journal 20(12): 2100-2107.

Andrews, M I, George, S and Joseph, J (2005) *Zoo's Print Journal* 20(6): 1889-1895.

Annamalai, R (2004) Biodiversity of Kalakad-Mundanthurai Tiger Reserve. Chennai, Tamil Nadu Forest Department.

Anonymous (2000) *Directory of Wildlife Protected Areas in India*. ENVIS Bulletin No 3(1), Dehra Dun, Wildlife Institute of India.

Arockiaswami, M (1956) *The Kongu Country*. Madras, Madras University Press.

Asian Elephant Research and Conservation Centre (1998) *The Asian Elephant in South India: a GIS database for conservation of Project Elephant Reserves*. Technical Report No 6.

Bala, T (2001) *Habitat Analysis of the Nilgiri Tahr (Hemitragus hylocrius Ogilby) in Palni using Remote Sensing and GIS*. MSc Thesis. Pondicherry, University of Pondicherry.

Basha, S C, Mohanan, C and Sankar (1997) (eds) *Teak*. Trichur, Kerala Forest Department and Kerala Forest Research Institute.

Basu, P (1997) *Current Science* 73(2): 173-179.

Bauer, A M and Das, I (1999) *Journal of South Asian Natural History* 4(2): 213-218.

Begum, V I R and Ismail, S A (2004) *Zoo's Print Journal* 19(3): 1394-1400.

Beck, B (1992) *Peasant society in Kongu:* A Study of the Right and Left Sub-castes in India. Vancouver, Univerity of British Columbia.

Bhat, A (2000) In: *Endemic Fish Diversity of the Western Ghats* (ed) A G Ponniah and A Gopalakrishnan. Lucknow, National Bureau of Fish Genetic Resources, 148-151.

Bhatta, G (1997) *Current Science* 73(2): 183-187.

Bhatta, G and Prashanth, P (2004) *Current Science* 87(3): 388-392.

Bhatta, G and Srinivasa, R (2004) *Zootaxa* 644: 1-8.

Bhupathy, S and Kannan, P (1997) *Status of Agamid Lizards in the Western Ghats of Tamil Nadu, India*. Coimbatore, Salim Ali Centre for Ornithology and Natural History.

Biju, S D (2001) *A Synopsis to the Frog Fauna of the Western Ghats, India*. Tropical Botanical Garden and Research Institute/Occasional Publication of the Indian Society for Conservation Biology.

Biju, S D (2003) *Current Science* 84(3): 283-284.

Biju, S D and Bossuyt, F (2003) *Nature* 425: 711-714.

Biju, S D and Bossuyt, F (2005a) *Current Science* 88(1): 175-178.

Biju, S D and Bossuyt, F (2005b) *Journal of Herpetology* 39(3): 349-353.

Biju, S D and Bossuyt, F (2005c) *Copeia* 1: 29-37.

Bossuyt, F (2002) *Journal of Herpetology* 36(4): 656-661.

Bossuyt, F and Milinkovitch, M C (2000) *Proceedings of the National Academy of Sciences (USA)* 97(12): 6585-6590.

Breeks, J W (1873) (ed) *An Account of the Primitive Tribes and Monuments of the Nilgiris*. London, India Museum.

Buchanan, F (1807) *A Journey from Madras through the countries of Mysore, Canara and Malabar (Vol 1-3)*. Cleveland Row, W Bulmer and Company.

Buchy, M (1996) *Teak and Arecanut: Colonial Forest and People in the Western Ghats (South India) 1800-1947*. Pondicherry, Institut Francais de Pondicherry and Indira Gandhi National Centre for Arts.

Champion, H G (1936) *Indian Forest Records* (ns) Silva I (1).

Dahaukar, N, Raut, R and Bhat, A (2004) *Journal of Biogeography* 31: 123-136.

Daniels, A E D (2003) *Studies on the Bryoflora of the Southern Western Ghats, India*. PhD Thesis, Tirunelveli, Manonmanian Sundraranar University.

Daniels, A E D and Daniel, P (2003) *Indian Journal of Forestry* 26(2): 193-194.

Daniels, R J R (1984) *Newsletter for Bird Watchers* 24 (9and10): 8-9.

Daniels, R J R (1989) *A Conservation Strategy for the Birds of the Uttara Kannada District*. PhD Thesis, Bangalore, Indian Institute of Science.

Daniels, R J R (1992) *Journal of Biogeography* 19: 521-529.

Daniels, R J R (1993) *Current Science* 64(10): 706-708.

Daniels, R J R (1994) *Blackbuck* 10(3and4): 61-70.

Daniels, R J R (1996a) *Ibis* 138: 64-69.

Daniels, R J R (1996b) 'The Nilgiri Biosphere Reserve: A Review of Conservation Status with recommendations for a Holistic Approach to Management'. UNESCO (South-South Cooperation Programme) Paris, Working Paper No 16.

Daniels, R J R (1997) *A Field Guide to the Birds of South-western India,* New Delhi: Oxford University Press.

Daniels, R J R (2001a) 'National Biodiversity Strategy and Action Plan –Western Ghats Eco-region', Report Submitted to the Ministry of Environment and Forests, Government of India.

Daniels, R J R (2001b) *Current Science* 81(3): 101-105.

Daniels, R J R (2001c) In: *Tropical Ecosystems: Structure, Diversity and Human Welfare* (ed) K N Ganeshaiah, R Uma Shaanker and K S Bawa, New Delhi, Oxford and IBH Publishing Co Pvt Ltd.

Daniels, R J R (2002) *Freshwater Fishes of Peninsular India.* Hyderabad: Universities Press.

Daniels, R J R (2003) *Current Science* 85(10): 1415-1422.

Daniels, R J R (2004) *Current Science* 87(8): 1030-1031.

Daniels, R J R (2005) *Amphibians of Peninsular India.* Hyderabad: Universities Press.

Daniels, R J R (2006a) *The Nilgiri Tahr: An Endemic South Indian Mountain Goat.* New Delhi, Macentimetreillan India Ltd.

Daniels, R J R (2006b) *Current Science* 90(4): 481.

Daniels, R J R, Hegde, M and Vinutha, C (1989) *J. Bombay Natural History Society* 86: 329-332.

Daniels, R J R, Joshi, N V and Gadgil, M (1990a) *Biological Conservation* 52: 37-48.

Daniels, R J R, Hegde, M and Gadgil, M (1990b) Proc. *Indian Acad. Sci. (Animal Sciences)* 99(1): 89-99.

Daniels, R J R, Hegde, M, Joshi, N V and Gadgil, M (1991) *Conservation Biology* 5(4): 464-475.

Daniels, R J R, Joshi, N V and Gadgil, M (1992) *Proceedings of the National Academy of Sciences (USA)* 89: 5311-5315.

Daniels, R J R, Gadgil, M and Joshi, N V (1995a) *J. Applied Ecology* 32: 866-874.

Daniels, R J R, Anil Kumar, N and Jayanthi, M (1995b) *Current Science* 68(5): 493-495.

Daniels, R J R and Jayanthi, M (1996) *Tropical Ecology* 37(1): 39-42.

Daniels, R J R and Saravanan, S (1998) *Newsletter for Birdwatchers* 38(3): 49-51.

Daniels, R J R and Vencatesan, J (1998) *Current Science* 75(4): 353-355.

Das, A, Krishnaswamy, J, Bawa, K S, Kiran, M C, Srinivas, V, Samba Kumar, V and Karanth, U (2006) *Biological Conservation* (in press).

Das, I (1985) *Indian Turtles: A field guide.* Calcutta, World Wildlife Fund-India.

Das, I (1997) *Hamadryad* 22: 32-45.

Das, I and Kunte, K (2005) *Journal of Herpetology* 39(3): 465-470.

Das, I and Ravichandran, M S (1998) *Hamadryad* 22: 89-94.

Davidar, E R C (1971) *Journal of the Bombay Natural History Society* 68(2): 347-354.

Davidar, E R C (1975) *Journal of the Bombay Natural History Society* 73: 143-148.

Davidar, E R C (1978) *Journal of the Bombay Natural History Society* 75: 815-844.

Devy, M S and Davidar, P (2001) *Current Science* 80(3): 400-405.

Duellman, W E and Trueb, L (1986) *Biology of Amphibians.* Baltimore and London, The John Hopkins University Press.

Dutta, S K (1997) *Amphibians of India and Sri Lanka (Checklist and Bibliography).* Bhubaneshwar, Odyssey Publishing House.

Dutta, S K and Ray, P (2000) *Hamadryad* 25(1): 38-44.

Easa, P S (1998) 'Survey of Amphibians and Reptiles in Kerala part of Nilgiri Biosphere Reserve'. KFRI Research Report No 148.

Easa, P S and Shaji, C P (1997) *Current Science* 73(2): 180-182.

Emiliyamma, K G and Radhakrishnan, C (2003) Zoo's Print Journal 18(1): 1264-1266.

ENVIS (1998) *Wildlife and Protected Areas.* Dehra Dun, Wildlife Institute of India.

Eswaran, R and Pramod, P (2005) Zoos' *Print Journal* 20 (8): 1939-1942.

French Institute (1997) *Endemic Tree species of the Western Ghats (India),* Pondicherry—Electronic Version/Compact Disc.

Gadagkar, R, Nair, P, Chandrashekara, K and Bhat, D M (1993) *Hexapoda* 5(2): 79-94.

Gadgil, M and Guha, R (1992) *This Fissured Land*. New Delhi, Oxford University Press.

Gadgil, M and Meher-Homji, V M (1986) *Proceedings of the Indian Academy of Science (Animal Sciences/Plant Sciences)* Supplement 165-180.

Ganesh, T and Davidar, P (1999) *J Tropical Ecology* 15: 399-413.

Ganesh, T, Ganesan, R, Devy, M S, Davidar, P and Bawa, K S (1996) *Current Science* 73(2): 188-194.

Gaonkar, H (1996) 'Butterflies of Western Ghats, India including Sri Lanka: a biodiversity assessment of a threatened mountain system'. Unpublished Report submitted to CES, Indian Institute of Science (Bangalore) and Zoological Museum, Copenhagen (Denmark) and Natural History Museum (London).

George, S, Martens, K and Nayar, C K G (1993) *Hydrobiologia* 254: 183-193.

George, S and Martens, K (1993) *J. Natural History* 27: 255-265.

Giller, P S and Malmqvist, B (1998) *The Biology of Streams and Rivers*. Oxford, Oxford University Press.

Giri, V, Wilkinson, M and Gower, D J (2003) *Zootaxa* 351: 1-10.

Giri, V, Gower, D J and Wilson, M (2004) *Zootaxa* 739: 1-19.

Gopalakrishnan, M (1995) (ed) *Gazetteers of India—Tamil Nadu State: The Nilgiris District*. Chennai, Government of Tamil Nadu, Commissioner of Archives and Historical Research.

Grimmett, R, Inskipp, C and Inskipp, T (1999) *Pocket Guide to the Birds of the Indian Subcontinent*. New Delhi, Oxford University Press.

Gupta, K M (1933) *The Land System in South India between ca. AD 800 and AD 1200*. Lahore, Motilal Banarasi Dass.

Gururaja, K V and Ramachandra, T V (2005) 'Integrated Approaches to Minimise Ambiguities in Anuran Description'. Unpublished Manuscript of a Paper presented at the 2nd National Conference of the Western Ghats Forum in December 2005.

Harrison, J (1999) *A Field Guide to the Birds of Sri Lanka*. United Kingdom, Oxford University Press.

Hedges, S B (2003) *Nature* 425: 669-670.

Heywood, V (1995) (ed) *Global Biodiversity Assessment*. Cambridge, United Nations Environment Programme and Cambridge University Press.

Hockings, P (1989) (ed) *Blue Mountains: the Ethnography and Biogeography of a South Indian region.* New Delhi, Oxford University Press.

Hora, S (1953) *Science Progress* 162: 245-255.

Hosagoudar, V B (2006) *Zoos' Print Journal* 21(12): 2495-2505.

Illakkuvanar (1963) *Tolkappiyyam in English. Madurai,* Kural Neri Publishing House.

Inger, R F, Shaffer, H B, Koshy, M and Badke, R (1984) *Journal of the Bombay Natural History Society* 84: 406-427 and 551-570.

Inger, R F, Shaffer, H B, Koshy, M and Badke, R (1987) *Amphibia-Reptilia* 8: 189-202.

Ishwar, N M and Das, I (1998) *J. Bombay Natural History Society* 95(3): 513-514.

Ishwar, N M, Chellam, R and Kumar, A (2001) *Current Science* 80(3): 413-418.

Iyyengar, R (1929) *Aalvarkal Kaalanilai* (Tamil). Chidambaram, Manikavasakar Noolagam.

Jaishree, M (2000) *Biodiversity and Gender Correlates of Food Security: a case study of Kolli Hills, Tamil Nadu.* PhD Thesis, Chennai, University of Madras.

Johnsingh, A J T (2001) *Current Science* 80(3): 378-388.

Kanamadi, R D, Nandihal, H N, Saidapur, S K and Patil, N S (1996) *J. Advanced Zoology* 17(2): 68-70.

Kapoor, V (2006) *Zoos' Print Journal* 21(12): 2483-2488.

Karanth, K P (2006) *Current Science* 90(6): 789-792.

Karanth, U (1985) *Primate Conservation* 6: 73-84.

Karanth, U (1997) In: Paola Manfredi (ed) In Danger. New Delhi, Ranthambore Foundation, 75-89.

Karanth, U and Sunquist, M E (1992) *J Tropical Ecology* 8: 21-35.

Karanth, U and Sunquist, M E (1995) *J Animal Ecology* 65: 439-450.

Krishnamurthy, R S and Kiester, A R (1998) *Current Science* 75(3): 283-291.

Krishnamurthy, S V, Manjunath, A V and Gururaja, K V (2001) *Current Science* 80(7): 6687-891.

Krishnan, R M and Davidar, P (1996) *J Biogeography* 23: 783-789.

Kumar, A (1997) In: Paola Manfredi (ed) *In Danger.* New Delhi, Ranthambore Foundation, 99-105.

Kumar, A and Yoganand, K (1999) *Distribution and Abundance of Small Carnivores in Nilgiri Biosphere Reserve, India.* ENVIS Bulletin-Wildlife and Protected Areas Vol 2(2): 74-86.

Kunte, K (2000) *Butterflies of Peninsular India.* Hyderabad, Universities Press.

Kunte, K, Joglekar, A, Ghate, U and Pramod, P (1999) *Current Science* 77(4): 577-586.

Kuramoto, M and Joshy, S H (2003) *Current Herpetology* 22(2): 51-60.

Kurup, B M, Manoj Kumar, T G and Radhakrishnan, K V (2005) *Journal of the Bombay Natural Histroy Society* 102(2): 195-197.

Leigh Jr, E G (1982) In: *Ecology of a Tropical Rain Forest: seasonal rhythms and long-term changes* (ed) Egbert G Leigh Jr, A Stanley Rand and D H Windsor. Washington DC, Smithsonian Press.

Lengerke, H J von and Blasco, F (1989) In: Paul Hockings (ed) *Blue Mountains: the ethnography and biogeography of a south Indian region.* New Delhi, Oxford University Press, 20-78.

Ludden, D (1985) *Peasant History in South India.* Princeton, Princeton University Press.

Maclean, C D (1885) *Manual of the Administration of Madras Presidency (Vol I and II).* Madras, Government Press.

Manickam, V S and Irudayaraj, V (1992) *Pteridophyte Flora of the Western Ghats–South India.* New Delhi, BI Publication Pvt Ltd.

Manoharan, T M, Biju, S D, Nayar, T S and Easa, P S (1999) *Silent Valley: whispers of reason.* Trivandrum, Kerala Forest Department and Kerala Forest Research Institute.

Mathew, K M (1969) *Records of the Botanical Survey of India XX.* Calcutta, Botanical Survey of India.

Menon, A G K (1999) *Checklist—Freshwater Fishes of India.* Zoological Survey of India. Occasional Paper No 175.

Menon, S and Bawa, K S (1997) *Current Science* 73(2): 134-145.

Ministry of Environment and Forests (1998) *Implementation of Article 6 of the Convention on Biological Diversity in India—National Report.* New Delhi, Government of India.

Mishra, C and Johnsingh, A J T (1998) *Biological Conservation* 86: 199-206.

Mukherjee, D, Bhupathy, S and Nixon, A M A (2005) *Current Science* 89(8): 1326-1328.

Mumbrekar, K D and Madhyasta, N A (2006) *Zoos' Print Journal* 21(6): 2295.

Muniappan, R and Viraktamath, C A (2006) *Current Science* 91(7): 868-870.

Murali, K S and Shetty, R S (2001) *Current Science* 80(5): 675-678.

Murthy, T S N (1985) *Records of the Zoological Survey of India*—Occasional Paper No 72: 1-51.

Muthuramkumar, S, Ayyappan, N, Parthasarathy, N, Mudappa, D, Shankar Raman, T R, Selwyn, A M and Pragasam, L A (2006) *Biotropica* 38 (2): 143-160.

Nair, M C, Rajesh, K P and Madhusoodanan, P V (2005) *Bryophytes of Wayanad in Western Ghats*. Calicut, Malabar Natural History Society.

Nair, N C and Daniel, P (1986) *Proc. Indian Acad. Sci.* (Anim. Sci/Plant Sci.) Supplement: 127-163.

Nameer, P O (1998) *Checklist of Indian Mammals*. Trichur, Kerala Forest Department.

Parthasarathy, N (2001) *Current Science* 80(3): 389-393.

Pascal, J P (1988) *Wet Evergreen Forests of the Western Ghats*. Pondicherry, French Institute.

PHCC (1988) Proceedings of the seminar on 'Conservation and Ecological Management of the Western Ghats through Land-use Planning' Kodaikanal, Palni Hills Conservation Council.

Piggott, S (1952) *Prehistoric India*. Harmondsworth, Penguin Books Ltd.

Pillai, K N S (1984) *The Chronology of Early Tamils*. New Delhi, Asian Educational Services.

Pillai, R S (1986) 'Silent Valley: physiography, fauna explorations and general observations on fauna'. *Records of the Zoological Survey of India* 84(1-4): 1-7.

Pillai, R S and Ravichandran, M S (1999) *Records of the Zoological Survey of India*—Occasional Papers No 172: 1-117.

Prabhakar, R (1994) *Resource Use, Culture and Ecological change: a case study of the Nilgiri hills of southern India*. PhD Thesis, Indian Institute of Science, Bangalore.

Pradhan, M S, Sharma, R M and Shanker, K (1997) *Mammalia* 61(3): 448-450.

Pramod, P, Daniels, R J R, Joshi, N V and Gadgil, M (1997a) *Current Science* 73(2): 156-162.

Pramod, P, Joshi, N V, Ghate, U and Gadgil, M (1997b) *Current Science* 73(2): 122-127.

Prasad, S N (1998) *Current Science* 75(3): 228-235.

Prasad, S N, Nair, P V, Sharatchandra, H C and Gadgil, M (1979) *J Bombay Nat His Soc* 75(3): 718-743.

Prasad, S N, Vijayan, L. Balachandran, S, Ramachandran, V S and Verghese, C P A (1998) *Current Science* 75(3): 718-743.

Prater, S H (1980) *The Book of Indian Animals. Mumbai,* Bombay Natural History Society.

Radhakrishna, B P (1991) *Current Science* 61(9and10): 641-647.

Radhakrishna, B P (1993) *Current Science* 64(11and12): 787-793.

Rai, S N (2000) *Productivity of Tropical Rainforests of Karnataka.* Dharwad, Punarvasu Publications.

Ramakrishnan, P S, Saxena, K G and Chandrashekara, U M (2000) (eds) *Conserving the Sacred for Biodiversity Management.* New Delhi, Oxford and IBH Publishing Co. Pvt. Ltd.

Ramamurthy, V (1986) *History of Kongu (Part I): Prehistoric period to 1300 AD.* Madras, International Society for Investigation of Ancient Civilization.

Raman, T R S, Joshi, N V and Sukumar, R (2005) *Journal of the Bombay Natural History Society* 102(2): 1-10.

Ramesh, B R, Menon, S and Bawa, K S (1997) *Ambio* 26(8): 529-536.

Rao, T A (1998) *Conservation of Wild Orchids of Kodagu in the Western Ghats.* New Delhi, World Wide Fund for Nature—India.

Ratheesh, N and Mohanan, C (2001) In: K N Ganeshaiah, R Umashaanker and K S Bawa (eds) *Tropical Ecosystems—Structure, Diversity and Human Welfare* (Supplement) New Delhi, Oxford and IBH Publishing Co. Pvt. Ltd.

Rice, C G (1984) *The Behaviour and Ecology of the Nilgiri Tahr.* PhD Thesis, Texas, A and M University.

Sasidharan, N (2000) *Forest trees of Kerala.* Peechi, Kerala Forest Research Institute.

Sastri, K A N (1976) *A History of South India—from prehistoric times to the fall of Vijayanagar (Fourth Edition).* New Delhi, Oxford University Press.

Selvamony, N (1989) *Tolkappiyam: akattinai iyal.* Nagercoil, Sobitham Publishers.

Shanker, K (2001) *Journal of Zoology (London)* 253: 15-24.

Shanker, K (2003) *Journal of the Bombay Natural History Society* 100(1): 46-57.

Shanker, K and Sukumar, R (1999) *Journal of Animal Ecology* 68: 50-59.

Sheeba, K K and Mohanan, C (2001) In: K N Ganeshaiah, R Umashaanker and K S Bawa (eds) *Tropical Ecosystems—Structure, Diversity and Human Welfare* (Supplement) New Delhi, Oxford and IBH.

Shetty, B V, Kaveriappa, K M and Bhat, K G (2002) *Plant Resources of Western Ghats and Lowlands of Dakshina Kannada and Udipi Districts.* Mangalore, Pilikula Nisarga Dhama Society.

Singh, D K (1997) In: V Mudgal and P K Hajra (ed) *Floristic Diversity and Conservation Strategies in India Vol I—Cryptogams and Gymnosperms.* Calcutta, Botanical Survey of India, 235-300.

Singh, D K (2002) *Notothylaceae of India and Nepal.* Dehra Dun, Bishen Singh Mahendra Pal Singh.

Sreekantha, Gururaja, K V, Rema Devi, K, Indra, T J and Ramachandra, T V (2006) *Zoos' Print Journal* 21(4): 2211-2216.

Srivastava, A and Srivastava, S C (2002) Indian Geocalcycaceae (Hepatiacae) (A Taxonomic Study). Dehra Dun, Bishen Singh Mahendra Pal Singh.

Stein, B (1971) Historical eco-types in south India. In: R E Asher (ed) *Proceedings of the II International Conference of Tamil Studies,* Madras: 284-288.

Subash Babu, K K and Nayar, C K G (2004) *Journal of the Bombay Natural History Society* 101(2): 296-298.

Subash Chandran, M D (1997) *Current Science* 73(25): 146-155.

Subramaniam, N (1968) *Sangam Polity: the administration and social life of the Sangam Tamils.* New York, Asia Publishing House.

Sukumar, R, Ramesh, R, Pant, R K and Rajagopalan, G (1993) *Nature* 364: 704-706.

Sunderraj, S F W and Johnsingh, A J T (2001) *Current Science* 80(3): 428-436.

Sureshan, P M, Yadav, B E and Radhkrishnan, C (2004) *Zoos' Print Journal* 19(3): 1401-1407.

Sureshan, P M, Khanna, V and Radhakrishnan, C (2006) *Zoos' Print Journal* 21(6): 2285-2291.

Swengel, F B (1991) *The Nilgiri Tahr Studbook.* USA, Minnesota Zoo.

Talwar, P K and Jhingran, A G (1991) *Inland Fishes—Vol II.* New Delhi, Oxford and IBH Publishing Co. Ltd.

Tikader, B K (1987) *Handbook: Indian Spiders*. Calcutta, Zoological Survey of India.

Tikader, B K and Bastawade, D B (1983) *Fauna of India—Arachnida Vol III: Scorpions*. Calcutta, Zoological Survey of India.

Vallinayagam, S, Manickam, V S and Seeni, S (2002) *Phytomorphology* 52(1): 23-27.

Vasanthy, C (1988) *Journal of Paleobotany and Palynology* 55: 175-192.

Vasudevan, K and Dutta, S K (2000) *Hamadryad* 25(1): 21-28.

Vasudevan, K, Kumar, A and Chellam, R (2001) *Current Science* 80(3): 406-412.

Vencatesan, J (2003) *Forest Reserves as Refugia for Human Impacted Biodiversity: a case study of the forest dynamics plot in Mudumalai Wildlife Sanctuary, India*. Unpublished report submitted to the Centre for Tropical Forest Studies of the Smithsonian Tropical Research Institute.

Vishnu-Mittre and Gupta, H P (1968) *Current Science* 37: 671-672.

Vohra, J N and Aziz, M N (1997) In: V Mudgal and P K Hajra (ed) Floristic Diversity and Conservation Strategies in India Vol I—*Cryptogams and Gymnosperms*. Calcutta, Botanical Survey of India, 301-374.

Zacharias, J (1999) 'Conceptualizing Extinction of Species: the macro-micro situation'. Unpublished MPhil Dissertaion submitted to the M G University, Kottayam.

F/RUP001/1645/07/08